The 28th *SS* Volunteer Grenadier Division '*Wallonien*', which consisted mostly of French-speaking citizens of the Kingdom of Belgium – first as part of the *Wehrmacht* and later in the ranks of the *Waffen-SS* – fought as one of the national legions against the Red Army on the Eastern Front in February 1942. The Walloons gained fame during the legendary resistance in the Cherkassy Pocket, where in early 1944 they lost more than 50 percent of their strength. In the summer of the same year they fought a defensive battle in Estonia in the region of Dorpat, and in February 1945 were directed to Western Pomerania, where until the last days of the war they put up a stubborn resistance to the armies of Stalin.

This book, which was originally published in Polish, is based on the unpublished memoirs of participants of these events, and is the first account to describe the Walloons' participation in the mysterious Pomeranian campaign in such a detailed manner. It tells the tragic story of the Walloon volunteers, who at all costs tried to stop the onrush of the enemy standing at the gates of the Third Reich. The Pomeranian odyssey, led by the controversial and infamous *Volksführer* Leon Degrelle, went on for three months, and the trial meant death and courage. Stargard, Altdamm, Neu-Rosow – these are locations, that became synonyms for unconditional sacrifice. They are also a symbol of *kameradschaft*, of a group of tough guys and dare-devils, who were determined to stake everything on one throw of the dice.

The book is illustrated with unique photographs, known so far only to a small group of people. These are complemented by a special comic created by the French artist Godus and with images made with great attention to detail, which were produced for historical reconstruction, showing silhouettes of the Walloon soldiers. It is worth noting that some of these were made in the same location where the fighting raged in April 1945.

Tomasz Borowski has been interested in history since childhood and for many years has been studying the actions of foreign volunteer formations of the *Waffen-SS* – especially Scandinavian, French and Walloon troops, which were involved in bloody battles in the final stages of the Second World War. His fascination arose when he realised how much influence these small, but extremely valiant and brave, troops had on the fate of the fronts on which they had to fight. They fought hard even though the cause for which they shed blood was practically lost.

Through contact with many authors and historians he has access to little-known archives, both of memoirs and of photographic material. In his publications, he tries not to repeat the well-known facts, but each time to bring closer and reveal to readers the mysteries and curiosities that are the symbols of the tragic last weeks of the greatest existing armed conflict, which for many has become a mythical 'Twilight of Gods'. He writes from a desire to tell stories. He believes that reading should primarily be a pleasure. If a story supposes to be boring, better not to show it to the world at all.

In his spare time the author watches criminal movies and good TV dramas such as 'Millennium', 'Sherlock' or 'True Detective'. Besides that he likes bike-riding, walking, spending time with his family and enjoying a glass of fine wine. He is also a cat enthusiast.

LAST BLOOD ON POMERANIA

LEON DEGRELLE AND THE WALLOON WAFFEN-*SS* VOLUNTEERS, FEBRUARY–MAY 1945

Tomasz Borowski

Translated by Monika Klimczak

Helion & Company

Helion & Company Limited
26 Willow Road
Solihull
West Midlands
B91 1UE
England
Tel. 0121 705 3393
Fax 0121 711 4075
Email: info@helion.co.uk
Website: www.helion.co.uk
Twitter: @helionbooks
Visit our blog http://blog.helion.co.uk/

Published by Helion & Company 2016
Designed and typeset by Farr out Publications, Wokingham, Berkshire
Cover designed by Paul Hewitt, Battlefield Design (www.battlefield-design.co.uk)
Printed by Henry Ling Limited, Dorchester, Dorset

Text © Tomasz Borowski 2015
Front cover: Ida Kozłowski
Images © as individually credited

ISBN 978-1-910294-48-2

British Library Cataloguing-in-Publication Data.
A catalogue record for this book is available from the British Library.

For details of other military history titles published by Helion & Company
Limited contact the above address, or visit our website: http://www.helion.co.uk.

We always welcome receiving book proposals from prospective authors.

Contents

List of Photographs and Maps

Maps

Colour photographs

Author's Note

The idea to tell the story of Walloon volunteers in the *Waffen-SS*, who fought in the Western Pomerania, came to me when I was commissioned to write an article about the life of one of them. I never would have imagined taking up such a challenge which, at first, seemed impossible. I admit that even when I had first contacted the Pomost ('Bridge') – my first publishing house in Poland, I was not altogether certain I would finish my work. I had hardly any sources to draw from and the literature on the subject is extremely poor. The subject I chose was rather broadly described only in unofficial publications which I was hard pressed to find on the book store shelves, internet auctions or antique book stores. The simple reason for that was the fact that these publications were printed only in small volume and for the benefit of a rather small group of readers, mostly the veterans of the *28th SS-Volunteer Grenadier Division 'Wallonien'*. Only after some time, since the decision to write on this subject, and thanks to the help of several friends, I was able to find the most fascinating sources I could draw from and finish this humble work.

I have to say this entire story became much more than just writing a book. It became rather a grand adventure, a kind of sanctuary I could retreat to and which helped me get through everyday difficulties and troubles.

For sure, I do not pretend to have the right to call myself a writer or a historian. Rather, I'm an aficionado who had the opportunity to discover a great many of the still unexplored secrets of those most exciting, if tumultuous and dark, last weeks of the Second World War.

I trust I was able to reflect the spirit of those days thanks to the memory material of the veterans who had survived that hell and thanks to my own, let's call it creative, imagination. I also hope this publication will serve as a remembrance of these simple Walloon soldiers who shed blood on foreign soil and that I will keep their memory alive. However controversial their history may be, even in their own homeland, these men surely deserve to be remembered.

At this point I would like to acknowledge the people who played a great part in the writing of this book and whom I wish to thank deeply:

My publisher Duncan Rogers, for his trust and for helping me realise one of my dreams.

My Polish publisher Maciej Karalus for support and help in the past years.

Michel le Roy, for his selfless assistance and singular support he gave me through all those months I worked. A great part of the unique photographs and veterans' recollections that came to light in this book did so due to his help.

Łukasz Dyczkowski and Dariusz Machalski from the Independent Photoreporters Association – Pathfinder of History (pol. *Tropiciel* Historii) for taking such excellent portraits of Walloon volunteers and for their help in promoting this project.

Aleksander Janik, Marek Łukasik and Michał Kołaczyk from the Historical Reenactment Group Pomerania 1945 for their participation in the photo shoot and their willingness to faithfully convey the spirit of the last days of *Kampfrugge* 'Derriks'.

The French master of drawings, Stephan Gosselin 'Godus' for his time and for creating, specially for me, the comic book which told the story of Walloon volunteers and their fight in Pomerania in such sharp strokes.

Charles Verpoorten for allowing me access to unique materials from his collection, for telling me the story of his father and for such a truly royal welcome at our meeting in Berlin.

Eddy de Bruyne for allowing me to use his research in my book and for his much appreciated advice.

And you, my Dear Reader, for deciding to buy this book. I hope the time you spend reading it will be a good one.

Finally, I'd like to thank my parents, Janina and Tadeusz, for everything. I believe my dad, who passed away before its publication, would have been proud of me as well as the book.

Poznań, November 2014.

For Monika S. without whom nothing would come to be ...

Je tiens tout d'abord à adresser mes plus vifs remerciements à Michel le Roy qui m'a soutenu d'une manière exceptionnelle et désinteressée tout au long de mon travail. La plupart des photographies uniques et souvenirs des anciens combattants, utilisés dans mon ouvrage, avaient été relevés grace à lui.

1

Beginnings

To tell the story of the 28th *SS*-Volunteer Grenadier Division *'Wallonien'* in Western Pomerania, one must first make a brief introduction and, at the very least, a sketch of the combat trail taken by this formation and their predecessors. We should also remember the political background and motivations which pushed the Walloon volunteers to stand with the Third Reich in this greatest global conflict of all time.

On 27 June 1941, the Nazi German leader, Adolf Hitler, gave his permission to create national legions in the occupied countries, which were to support the German war effort in their fight against the Soviet Union. Belgium created two such formations: one comprising of the inhabitants of Flanders and one comprising of the French-speaking Walloons.[1] The Flemish, with their Nordic origins, have been recognised by the *SS* Head Office as Aryan enough and thus were incorporated into the *Waffen-SS*. The Walloon troops became part of the *Wehrmacht*.

Among the Walloon right-wing activists Leon Degrelle was the greatest proponent of cooperation with the Germans. Having left the ranks of the Belgian Catholic Party, he became the head of the People's Rexist Movement 'Christus Rex', a movement he himself had founded in 1935.

From its very beginnings Rexism appeared to be a nonconformist and anti-systemic movement, denouncing any political affiliations. Its ideology was a complete novelty on the political scene of the time. Its goals were not the recreation of the government in accordance to any programme line, but rather a kind of spiritual revolution. In short, Rexism was about aversion to materialism; it was about youth empowerment and a deep Catholic mysticism in the spiritual sphere.[2] In the first year since their establishment, by democratic mechanisms, Rexists managed to gain close to 12 percent of the votes and put as many as 29 representatives in the Belgian Parliament. Before 1939, they had almost one-third

---

1 Bishop, Chris, *Zagraniczne Formacje SS* (Warsaw: Muza, 2008), p. 31 (all footnotes, unless indicated otherwise, are from the author).
2 Degrelle, Leon, *Płonące Dusze* (Warsaw, 2011), p. 8.

1.   Leon Degrelle in uniform of the *Formations de Combat* and in front of
his villa – Dreve de Lorraine in Brussels. (J.L. Roba's collection)

of all the votes in some of the Belgian regions.[3] They managed to achieve all that
largely due to activities such as organising holidays for the children of the workers
or by directing young female members, from wealthy homes mostly, to help out
the worker families. This also allowed them to experience problems which were
foreign to them such as poverty, homelessness and hunger, etc.[4]

After the German invasion of Belgium on 10 May 1940, around 1,000 Rexist
activists, alongside their leader Leon Degrelle, were arrested and turned over
to the French.[5] They were released however after the French-German ceasefire.
Quite possibly this is the moment when talks with the occupant begin in order
to maintain the institutional unity of the Belgium Kingdom.[6] From the German

3   Ladriere, Jean, *La Decision Politique en Belgique* (Brusseles, 1965), pp. 85, 86.
4   Degrelle, op. cit., p. 9.
5   Degrelle was actually a supporter of Belgium's neutrality and was as opposed to the idea of 'dying for
Gdańsk' as he was opposed to the communists. One of the reasons for the Rexists being arrested was
that they had remained in active contact with the NSDAP. Degrelle himself had attended the party's
conventions in the past. (ed.)
6   In the context of international law, German occupation could not change Belgium's legal status or
its institutional unity. The talks, then, could only concern the division of occupied Belgium from a
legalistic point of view. Belgium was to be divided into separate territorial units run by the Germans.
Belgium is a country of two nationalities: the Flemish in the North (Flanders), with their own unique
language, and the French-speaking Walloons in the South. Degrelle was pushed to cooperation with

2.   Members of the Rexist Party: Raymond Noirfalise (killed by the resistance on 19 May 1944) and Mathias Brossel (killed by a sniper on the Eastern Front on 11 June 1942). (Michel le Roy's collection)

point of view, the most valuable assets of the Rexist movement were, undoubtedly, their paramilitary battle troops known as *Formations de Combat*, as well as their prevention forces *Brigade Vollante Rex*, also known as the airborne brigades. The youth organisation of *Les Serments de La Jeunesse Rexistes* and its female off-shoot *Les Femmes Rexistes* should also not be forgotten.[7]

After 22 June 1941, once the war with the Soviet Union had begun, the idea of a struggle against international Communism became even more alive among the European nationalists, including the Walloons. By Leon Degrelle's initiative and under the leadership of his second-in-command, Fernand Ruleau, 'Corps Franc Wallonie' was created, soon to be renamed as '*Legion Belge Wallonie*'. Ultimately the name was changed into '*Legion Wallonie*'.[8] The soldiers who served in the Belgian Army before the war were allowed to keep their ranks. Among others,

---

the Germans by collaborative demands from separatist groups: the German-Flemish Working Group (*Devlag*), who wanted Flanders to be incorporated into the Reich, and the Flemish National Union, who demanded Flanders to become a part of the 'New Netherlands'. (ed.)

7   Littlejohn, David, *Foreign Legions of the Third Reich,* vol. 2 (R. James Bender Publishing, 1987), pp. 87–88.

8   Bishop, op. cit., p. 31.

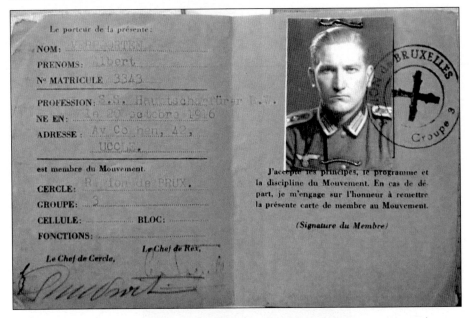

3.   Albert Verpoorten's party membership card. (Charles Verpoorten's collection)

three representatives of the Belgian aristocracy served in that formation, which quickly grew to 900 soldiers, including also a couple of Russian White Guards, who fought the Bolsheviks during the Civil War after the Russian revolution.[9]

On 8 August, the unit received its battle call-sign: the 373rd Walloon Infantry Battalion – *'Wallonische Infanterie-Bataillon 373'*. It is noteworthy that Degrelle, despite his assuredly privileged position due to his political work, joined the ranks as a private.[10]

SS-Obergruppenführer Felix Steiner, who was later to command the Walloon volunteers in battle, characterised Degrelle in following words:

> The Walloon Legion had the sharpest national profile among all foreign troops. It seemed to focus all the characteristic features of the Walloons, but it was also engaged in realising some very far-reaching national goals, by means of military partnership with Germany. The Legion was more than just a military unit. It was also a political force, gathered around its spiritual leader – Leon Degrelle. He served in the Legion as a simple private, but then advanced to the

---

9   Ibid., p. 33.
10   Degrelle did so in protest against his removal from political leadership over the Walloon Legion, which took place while he was travelling to occupied France in the autumn of 1944. Later, on the front, thanks to his considerable skill with propaganda and his charisma, he was able to regain unquestioned political leadership over the legion. (ed.)

4.   The Walloon Volunteers' contingent's departure to the
front on 10 March 1942. (Michel le Roy's collection)

rank of a non-commissioned officer, then a commissioned officer, ultimately becoming a commander in the rank of general. He was a typical Walloon: ambitious, courageous, and a magnanimous enthusiast. He was quick to share his infectious passion, was always the dare-devil. [...] Convinced that the Walloon combat prowess was the best guarantee of a better future for Belgium, he was very serious in his devotion to the military tasks. Understanding and knowing his men, Degrelle was very passionate in imbuing them with a sense of a soldier's honour and encouraged them to perform heroic deeds. His honest pro-social attitude opened the hearts of his legionnaires. Although these soldiers came from all layers of society, most of them were young workers who had complete trust in their commander and persevered at his side until the very end of the war.[11]

The words above seem to perfectly represent the motivations of hundreds of young Walloon nationalists who chose to shed blood on the Eastern Front. They truly believed that should the Third Reich achieve victory (which appeared more

---

11   Steiner, Felix, *Ochotnicy Waffen SS. Idea I Poświęcenie* (Gdańsk, 2010), pp. 86-87.

5.   Volunteers of the Walloon Legion during assembly with their first banner. (Michel le Roy's collection)

6.   Leon Degrelle during a march through a Russian village. (Charles Verpoorten's collection)

than probable at the end of 1941), their country would become a nation equal to Germany on the map of the 'New Europe' under the guide of Adolf Hitler. Also, one cannot discount that youthful dare-devil streak in some of them, as well as their thirst for adventure.

The first volunteers completed their training on 15 October 1941, and by the end of that month the decision was made to send them to the front.[12] Because the Legion was too small a formation to fight on its own, the Germans tasked them with the protection of communication lines in the Dniepropietrovsk region in the Ukraine. The soldiers, serving under Captain Pierre Pauly, first clashed with the Red Army in February of 1942,[13] having been ordered to push the Soviets out of the village of Gromovayabalka.[14] The battle was largely close quarters and the Walloons paid heavily in lives. The unit lost almost 50 percent of its original number, which dropped to less than 250 combat-ready soldiers. On 2 March, the formation was relieved by German troops. For his courage on the battlefield, Degrelle was raised to the rank of *Oberfeldwebel* (a sergeant), and the Legion proved its battle-worthiness. After a few weeks of rest, having replenished its ranks and returning to the original number (circa 500-600), the Legion was back at the Eastern Front, where in May 1942 it was incorporated into the 97th Infantry Division (*97th Infanterie Division*).[15] By that time, the command of the troop was given to an experienced artillery man, Major Lucien Lippert, who replaced Captain Georges Tchekoff, a former Tsarist navy officer.

In the summer of 1942, the Walloon Battalion fought over the Don. In autumn, it moved to the Caucasus to cover supply lines, taking part only in minor battles. During the fighting near Tuapse, in Krasnodar Krai, the Walloons fought alongside the 5th *SS-Panzergrenadier* Division *'Wiking'*.[16] In that time,

---

12 It is probable that during training, the Walloon troops were assigned to the occupying forces in the region, which was a common practice in the German military. From August to December of 1941 the battalion took part in anti-Partisan actions within the General Government. Any charges of war crimes committed by the Legion's soldiers during the time, as well as during anti-Partisan operations on the Soviet Union's territory in 1942, remain unknown. (ed.)

13 The battalion was then incorporated into the 100th Light Infantry Division (*Leichte Infanterie-Division*). (ed.)

14 Bishop, op. cit., p. 35.

15 Before that, however, it had joined the 68th Infantry Division and only then – the 97th Light Infantry Division. The names of the 97th and the 100th Light Infantry Division commonly used in the literature (Infantry Division, Mountain Division, Mountain Gunnery Division) are incorrect. All light infantry divisions (including the 97th and the 100th) changed their names on 6 July 1942 into Gunnery Divisions (*Jäger-Divisionen*). These divisions had a special complement of two regiments which made them more operative and cohesive during certain combat operations. Perhaps it is that experience, gathered in these special divisions, which may be the reason for the Walloon Division's unusual two-regiment structure – that and the lack of recruits, of course. (ed.)

16 Solarz, Jacek, *Wiking 1941-1945* (Warsaw, 2003), p. 33.

7.   Walloon Legionnaires resting after battle in Caucasus. Albert
Verpoorten is first on the right. (Charles Verpoorten's collection)

8.   Legionnaires on the march. (Charles Verpoorten's collection)

9. Roger Lejeune: an officer and a dentist in the Walloon Legion. After the war, he was sentenced to prison for collaboration. Having escaped the prison, he spent the remainder of his life in emigration in Spain. (Michel le Roy's collection)

Leon Degrelle (already promoted to Lieutenant) was supposed to connect with the division's commander, the aforementioned Felix Steiner, and now, enthused by the *Waffen-SS* ethos, he started to instil the formation's particular ideological fervour into his own men.[17]

Felix Steiner describes the battle for Tuapse in following words:

Finally, at the beginning of October, the attack on Tuapse had commenced. The charge turned into a difficult struggle in the mountains, valleys and forests, over streams and on mountain paths, where more often we had to carve our way with axes, saws and shovels, than actually fight with heavy weapons. [...] The Legionnaires, lacking the proper specialist alpine equipment, followed their division. [...] Hepatitis, pneumonia and bloody losses decimated their ranks. Shallow dugouts did not provide sufficient protection from elements. Supplies

17 Bishop, op. cit., p. 36.

begun to fail as well. The Legionnaires suffered cold and hunger. When they were finally relieved, their mountain-troop career came to an end. Of the thousand men who crossed the Donets, barely two hundred marched back to the west.[18]

---

18   Steiner, op. cit., p. 121.

2

Under the SS Banner

After the fighting in Caucasus, the majority of the sub-units (with the exception of only one of the Legion's companies) returned to Belgium for convalescence and to replenish their numbers.[1] Meanwhile, Leon Degrelle was summoned to Berlin in order to discuss the perspectives for the future growth of the Walloon volunteer formation. Using his reputation and fame, he managed to reach an agreement with the *SS-Reichsführer* Heinrich Himmler and the chief of the *SS* Head Office (*SS-Hauptamt*) Gottleb Berger. The agreement was to that the Legion would become part of the *Waffen-SS*, which happened on 1 June 1943.[2] The 373rd *Wehrmacht* Infantry Battalion officially became the *SS*-Volunteer Assault Brigade 'Wallonien' (*SS-Freiwilligen-Sturmbrigade 'Wallonien'*) and was sent to the proving grounds in Wildflecken for training. Lucien Lippert, now in the rank of *SS-Sturmbannführer*, kept command of the brigade. Leon Degrelle, advanced to the rank of *SS-Hauptsturmführer*, became his second-in-command. It is a curious fact that a Catholic chaplain served in the unit, which was a rarity in the 'Germanic *SS* order'. This becomes less surprising when taking into account that many of the old Legionnaires, including Degrelle himself, were fervent Catholics.[3]

Having completed their training and the organisational tasks necessary in the course of forming the unit, in the middle of November, the brigade was deployed to the Ukraine to join back with the *'Wiking'* Division. In January of 1944, the brigade crushed a Soviet advance line at Teklino. The victory was short-lived however, since on 26 January the Soviet 6th Tank Army broke the front and surrounded about 56,000 German soldiers.[4] In literature, the manoeuvre is known as the 'Cherkassy Cauldron'. The Germans made numerous attempts to push through the encirclement from outside, but to no avail. Finally they decided to break it from the inside. The Walloons fought to break the Soviet ring, serving as a kind of rearguard for their comrades from the *'Wiking'*. During their retreat,

---

1   Bishop, Chris, *Zagraniczne Formacje SS* (Warsaw: Muza, 2008), p. 36.
2   Ibid.
3   Landwehr, Richard, *The Wallonien – The History of...* (Bennington, 2006), p. 6.
4   Ibid., p. 175.

11.   A propaganda poster encouraging enlistment into the Assault Brigade '*Wallonien*'. (J.L. Roba's collection)

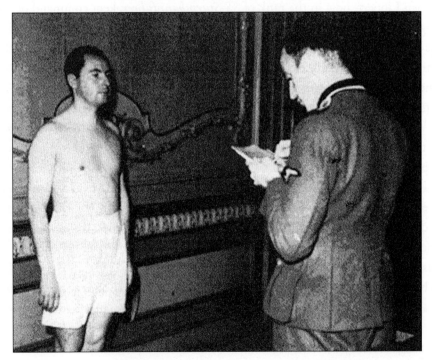

10.   Leon Degrelle during an examination by the medical board before his enlistment into the SS-Assault Brigade '*Wallonien*'. (*Axe & Allies* Magazine)

13.   Despite the difficult battles in the Ukraine, the Burgundians
      kept up their good spirits. (Eddy de Bruyne's collection)

12.   Walloon soldiers of the *SS* Brigade in the early stages of
      the fighting in Cherkassy. (J.L. Roba's collection)

14.   Leon Degrelle with his children and officers during a parade commemorating their return from the Cherkassy Cauldron. (J.L. Roba's collection)

15.   Walloon volunteers who survived the siege in Cherkassy. The photograph was taken on 1 April 1944 during the formation's parade through Charleroi. (*39-45* Magazine)

the Assault Brigade *'Wallonien'* suffered heavy losses. Among the fallen was its commander: *SS-Obersturmführer* Lucien Lippert, who was killed on 15 February 1944 near the town of Nova-Buda. Of the 1,500 Walloons who had fought at the start of the battle in the cauldron, less than 630 remained, which makes less than half of their original complement. In recognition of his merit during the fighting in the cauldron, Leon Degrelle was awarded the Knight's Cross of the Iron Cross.

The remaining Walloon survivors were sent back to Wildflecken to rest and to replenish their numbers. Thanks to their heroic efforts at the battle in Cherkassy, and the surrounding propaganda campaign, a great many new volunteers enlisted in the brigade. The celebratory parades in Brussels, the Belgium capital, and in Charleroi reverberated throughout the country.

During the regrouping in Wildflecken, the brigade received a new tactical number, becoming the *5th SS-Sturmbrigade 'Wallonien'*. On 30 June 1944, their rank and file reached the following numbers:

• 43 officers

• 232 NCOs

• 903 privates

Altogether 1,188 soldiers – while the required full complement for a brigade was 2,500.[5]

After the start of the Battle of Narva, Estonia, known as the 'Battle of the European *SS*', a select battalion, in the force of 440 Walloons, marched to the northern segment of the front to defend the Tannenburg Line.[6] As a part of the 3rd *SS Panzer* Corps (Germanic), the Belgians tried to stop Soviet attacks on Tartu or Pskov. On 10 August, the unit joined the *SS-Kampfgruppe 'Wagner'* and spent three weeks repelling Soviet tanks and infantry assaults.

By the end of the month, the Walloon group was left with just 200 soldiers who managed to avoid getting surrounded near the Estonian port of Tallin. In that time, *SS-Untersturmführer* Leon Gillis was awarded the Knight's Cross of the Iron Cross for single-handedly destroying a dozen or so tanks during the retreat. The order made Gillis the second, after Degrelle, recipient of this highest German commendation.[7] Degrelle, on his part, received a commendation in the Wolf's Lair at the hands of Adolf Hitler himself: the Oak Leaves for his Knight's Cross.[8] The award came in recognition of his leadership in the Battle of Narva.

---

5   Landwehr, op. cit., p. 29.

6   Considering the participation of volunteers from Denmark, Norway, Flanders or the Netherlands.

7   Littlejohn, David, *Foreign Legions of the Third Reich,* vol. 2 (R. James Bender Publishing, 1987), p. 117.

8   The Oak Leaves were awarded to soldiers who had previously received the Knight's Cross.

16.   Degrelle with one of his men: Tartu region, August 1944. (Michel le Roy's collection)

17.   Mortar crew in preparations for shelling: the front over
Narva, 1944. (Eddy de Bruyne's collection)

After the battle, the remnants of the formation were sent to Wrocław, then Hanover and Brunswick, where the brigade underwent yet another transformation – into the 28th *SS*-Volunteer Grenadier Division *'Wallonien'* (*28th SS-Freiwilligen Grenadier Division 'Wallonien'*).[9]

Enlistment begun on 20 September 1944. The division's complement, aside from veterans and new recruits from southern Belgium, included a number of French or even Spanish soldiers, formerly of the famous Blue Division (*'Division Azul'*), which fought earlier in the USSR on the Eastern Front.[10] A number of its members chose not to heed their government's call to lay down arms and did not retreat behind the Pyrenees. Wanting to continue their fight with Bolshevism, they joined the *Waffen-SS*.

In December of 1944, a part of the *'Wallonien'*, under Leon Degrelle's command, was deployed in the Ardennes, a region just taken by Sepp Dietriech's 6th *SS Panzer* Army. German high command planned to send both of the Belgian *SS* divisions, the 27th Flemish *'Langemarck'* and the 28th *'Wallonien'* back home. After the offensive in the Ardennes succeeded and the German forces took back the country, the divisions were to police and protect the region. That victory obviously never happened, so in the second half of January 1945 the Walloons received an order to gather all combat-ready soldiers into one battle-worthy operations group. They were to operate on the wobbling Eastern Front. The Walloons brought together some 4,000 men, who were divided into two regiments: the 69th under *SS-Sturmbannführer* Frans Hellebaut and the 70th under *SS-Sturmbannführer* Jules Mathieu.[11] It is no mystery that their respective complements met the division's requirements only on paper.

By most accounts, the command of the unit was in Leon Degrelle's hands. On 1 January 1945, Degrelle was promoted to *SS-Obersturmbannführer*. Richard Landwehr takes an interesting view on the matter. In reference to a book by Hugh

---

9   The division was supposed to be a standard infantry formation known in the *Waffen-SS* as grenadiers. Very often in historical studies, one may see an incorrect name – the 28th Volunteer *Panzergrenadier* Division *'Wallonien'* – which would suggest the unit was mechanised. In reality it was comprised of two incomplete *SS* grenadier regiments (the 69th and 70th) and of incomplete divisional units (number 28). The full third regiment, the 71st, never even began to form. (ed.)

10 Formed by Spanish volunteers in the summer of 1941, *'Division Azul'* went to the Eastern Front as the 250th *Wehrmacht* Infantry Division. During two years of fighting, almost 50,000 of Spanish volunteers had went through the division. On 16 November 1943, it was withdrawn and replaced by the so-called *'Legion Azul'* (1,500 – 2,000 soldiers). Ultimately, the Spanish troops fell back to the Iberian Peninsula in April of 1944 and the *'Division Azul'* was formally decommissioned on 25 April 1944. The volunteers, who refused the order to return, risked having their Spanish citizenship taken from them. (ed.)

11 Landwehr, op. cit., p. 33.

18.   Leon Degrelle in Prague, 11 December 1944. (Michel le Roy's collection)

Page Taylor, *Uniforms, History and Organisation of the Waffen-SS*, Landwehr argues that originally the commander of the formation was actually Nicolaus Heilmann (one of the 15th Grenadier Division's officers) who, promoted to *SS-Brigadeführer*, replaced Degrelle at the post. However, as soon as the Walloons had arrived in Pomerania, Heilmann was killed and Degrelle once again, and this time for good, took command.[12] Landwehr's hypothesis is not confirmed by any other sources known to the author and so it should be regarded with a large grain of salt.

Abel Delannoy,[13] one of the *'Wallonien's'* platoon leaders, a witness and participant of these events, speaks with eloquence of the last two days before deployment:

---

12   Ibid., p. 34.
13   Abel Delannoy was born on 17 December 1925 in Wasmuel. He served in the *'Wallonien'* Division from 1 April 1943 to 2 May 1945. Sentenced to 15 years of forced labour and a 100,000 F compensation fine for the 'moral damages suffered by the Belgian State', he was cleared of all charges in 1956. Later on, he worked as a miner and a labourer in a rolling-stock.

The Holidays of 1944/45 find our legion on icy roads at the back of the Western Front, near Duren. If anyone would ask us, we'd say: 'All quiet on the Western Front!'. The companies move under the cover of the dark, allied air force is much too active during the day. 'Till morning, the Burgundians march from quarters to quarters, never understanding the reason of all these movements.[14] The Front is still far away, we can only see the trajectories of launching V2s, seeking their targets hundreds of kilometres away. Our underfed horses are even more miserable than we are. Because the way is so slippery, we help them by carrying the shafts and finally unhitching them. We end up dragging these bloody carts and heavy infantry wagons ourselves. Our average speed is two kilometres per hour. A true *blitzkrieg* indeed! One of my comrades, whom we called 'Rake of Neweklau' for a reason, was named the commandants' second. His particular affinity for administrative positions seemed to confirm the choice. He would prepare our marching orders, in five points, never missing a single comma. He will pass us soon, politely waving goodbye from his motorcycle. Splendour and civility, military style! Seeing how exhausted we were by all this constant marching and counter-marching, our commander finally sent us to the East. We were to reinforce a gap in the widespread front-line, in the Pomerania. Russian tanks gallop through the land like crazy. Town empty quickly. Wagons filled with refugees pile up into long columns on the roads. Retreating colonists of old, who came here from our land centuries ago, namely: *'Naar Oostland willen wij nijjden naar. Oostland willen wil gaan'*.[15] Ever since the esteemed Ilia Gregorovich Erenburg chose to raise mass rape to a form of art, Germanic women realised that their only chance of survival lay behind a wall of chests of the sons of the West![16]

The 28th *SS*-Volunteer Grenadier Division had left the Niederaussem-Rheydt region at the end of January and after a couple days' journey by train reached Szczecin on 6 February 1945. Almost immediately they were shipped to Stargard Szczeciński [Stargard in Pommern] to defend a front-line endangered by the Soviet winter offensive, which had begun on 12 January. This is how Leon Degrelle remembers those first moments after arrival:

---

14 The Burgundians were Germanic people from Bornholm. In the 5th century, along with many other Germanic tribes, they settled on the territories of the Roman Empire by the Upper Rhine. Their history became the source for the famous 'Song of Nibelungs', which was one of the favourite Germanic myths for the nationalist movements. (ed.)

15 To the Western lands we wish to go, to the West we wish to go – a Dutch song.

16 Delannoy, Abel, *Confession d'un SS*, pp. 35-36.

19.   *SS-Untersturmführer* Abel Delannoy – leader of the 3rd Platoon in the
2nd Company of *Kampfgruppe 'Derriks'* – during fighting around Stargard.
Here he is in the rank of *SS-Sturmmann*. (Michel le Roy's collection)

Stargard was the last big city left to conquer on that trail. It was barely thirty-five kilometres away from the Lower Oder. On the morning of 6 February 1945, when we had arrived, the situation seemed hopeless. Russian tanks were attacking the city from the south-east, the south and the south-west. The city's defences were non-existent and in the hands of old-timers from *Volkssturm*, who did what they could but they were more prone to coughing fits than to victory.[17]

Below is Abel Delannoy's recollection:

My wretched battalion, as usual, had to make the way from Szczecin to Stargard on foot. Riding on a staff motorcycle with the speed of 80 km/h, I moved ahead. We found quarters in Schöneberg, a luxury sea-side Gut,[18] belonging to a prince, who served as the town's mayor. Before he left, he had invited the officers to dinner. The house keeper served the guests, wearing white gloves.

17   Degrelle, Leon, *Front Wschodni 1941-1945* (Międzyzdroje, 2002), p. 301.
18   Estate.

20.   With a microphone, on the left, is Franz Thiry. Victor Matthys is in a Rexist Party uniform; then pictured is Albert Verpoorten and Leon Degrelle. This photograph was most likely taken at the end of February 1944. (Charles Verpoorten's collection)

The host addressed her as '*Mam'zele*' (Mademoiselle). The custom probably originated from Prussia, the times of Voltaire and the Great King! A swansong of the feudal era, which allowed Europe to return to western markets. While searching for quarters for my men, I had a delightful guide. Even though she wasn't blond, she lacked for nothing. Anni was a hot brunette. She remained in Schoneberg to operate the telephone exchange. I was just about to say goodbye at her doorstep and take my leave, when she smiled at me so sweetly I couldn't help myself and I kissed her. Blimey! That kiss smelled of ripe peaches, what am I saying, it was a kiss smelling of wild strawberries. Such a kiss could've been the start of a beautiful feeling, my duties however did not allow for moonlit walks with Anni, which is the custom of those madly in love. Anni left the village. I wrote to her faithfully up until the day a friend of mine, Cremer from the TTR – damn those staff blaggers![19] – all in laughs, revealed his meaning laden secret: 'Anni, hi hi, ha ha! I kept her company during the evacuation all the way to Stargard![20]

19   *Troupe Transition*, special battalions within a division. Delannoy probably means the staff company.
20   Delannoy, op. cit., p. 37.

3

First Blood

On 15 January, the forces of the 1st Belorussian Front broke through German defences, splitting them in two. On the 31st, the 2nd Guards Tank Army and the 5th Shock Army reached the Oder near Kostrzyn.[1] At the beginning of February 1945, the Pomeranian front-line run through Chojnice [Konitz] – Wałcz [Deutsch Krone] – Pyrzyce [Pyritz] all the way to Oder by Schwedt. While the 1st Belorussian Front moved to Oder, Marshal Rokossovsky's 2nd Belorussian Front was to take the Pomerania in order to eliminate the threat from German troops, which still had the ability to strike at the West-bound right wing of Marshal Zhukov's 1st Belorussian Front.[2] To combat the increasing pressure exerted by the Red Army, since the start of February all German forces were being deployed to Pomerania, often at the cost of other, equally frayed, battle theatres.[3] Among those units who arrived on the Western frontier of the German Reich was the 28th *SS*-Volunteer Grenadier Division *'Wallonien'*.

The following Walloon forces engaged in the fighting on the banks of River Ina:

- 'Derriks' Battalion (I/69) to defend Krepcewo [Kremzow]
- 'Lakaie' Battalion (II/69) to defend Kolin [Kollin] and Strzebielewo [Streblow]
- 'Denie' Battalion (three companies from the I Battalion and the 70th *SS*-Grenadier Regiment) to defend Krąpiel [Schoneberg]
- Two companies of anti-tank and anti-aircraft guns
- One reconnaissance company

---

1 Tachoń, Jerzy, *Wojenne Okruchy*, [in:] *Stargardia*, vol. 2 (Stargard, 2002), p. 1.
2 Michaelis, Rolf, *Nordland* (Warsaw, 2004), p. 57.
3 In practice, the Soviet January offensive on the Pomerania created a gaping hole in the German front-line. The Germans tried to fill that hole by creating on 21 January 1945 the new Army Group 'Vistula'. The Group's CO was a military dilettante *SS-Reichsführer* Heinrich Himmler. As the leader of the *SS* and the commander of the *Wehrmacht* Reserve Army, he was believed by Hitler to be the best guarantee for the immediate and successful formation of the new army group by reaching for the available reserves. Indeed, Himmler managed to fill the Army Group 'Vistula' with a great number of *Waffen-SS* troops, including the Walloon Division, which was deployed to the Western Pomerania. (ed.)

21.   The road to Krępcewo [Kremzow] and Strzebielewo [Streblow]. The photograph shows the terrain the Burgundians had to fight in. (Tomasz Borowski)

22.   The train station in Kolin [Kollin]. (Tomasz Borowski)

23.   The Ina's tributary – the so-called 'Lazy Ina' – flowing
through Kolin [Kollin]. (Tomasz Borowski)

Altogether, about 1,800–2,000 soldiers were supported by the 10th SS *Panzer* Division *'Frundsberg'* on their right flank and the Flemish 27th *SS*-Volunteer Grenadier Division *'Langemarck'* on the left.[4] By Abel Delannoy's account, his division's anti-tank artillery functioned mainly in theory:

> Our convoy stopped in Szczecin. As the battalion's interim staff officer authorised for motor transport, I made contact with the general who quickly organised the sector's defences. He was ecstatic when he heard about the 28th *SS*-Division *'Wallonien's'* arrival. The Where's-your-artillery Division! They are artillery-men but no guns. The tides of war turned so fast, the Walloon *Volksgrenadierdivision* had no time to finish training or to acquire the proper equipment. We're going to have to stick with the infantry 'till the end of the war. On 8 August 1941, our predecessors had started likewise. The general was so disappointed! Had he never read Schiller? Artillery or not: *'Respekt fur ihn, es is ein Wallone!'*[5] The general turned out to be a dilettante, but putting his story aside, it is worth to note that the Szczecin railway station also welcomed

4   de Bruyne, Eddy, Rikmenspoel, Mark, *For Rex and Belgium ...* (Solihull, 2004), p. 284.
5   'Respect him, he is Walloon!' (German).

24.   The architecture of Kurcewo [Krussow]. The village has
not changed much since the war. (Tomasz Borowski)

a train full of young German women to operate the anti-aircraft batteries! A
couple of *Luftwaffe* reservists took care of them. Not too much though, I hope,
otherwise a heart-attack was a guarantee![6]

The enemy artillery fire quickly squashed those few localised attacks the
Walloons had tried. On 12 February 1945, the Soviet tanks appeared near Kurcewo
[Krussow]. In order to stop the degrading situation, the 5th Company from the
II/69 (2nd Battalion of the 69th *SS*-Regiment) temporarily removed the danger
of creating a hole in the Walloon defence lines. Their resistance, however, came
at the cost of the company commander's life, *SS-Untersturmführer* Rudi Bal.[7] At
this point, we should mention the fact that the authors of *For Rex and Belgium*
were most likely mistaken in their account of Rudi Bal's death. According to Jean
Mabire – and many valuable recollections of one of the division's veterans, who
fought in Pomerania, *SS-Untersturmführer* Roland Devresse – Bal was killed
in action on 6 March 1945 during the fighting near Lubowo [Lubow] and that
precise date should be counted as an official one.

In the meantime, the 1st and 3rd Companies from the II/70 (consisting

6   Delannoy, Abel, *Confession d'un SS*, p. 36.
7   de Bruyne, Rikmenspoel, op. cit., p. 285.

mostly of Spanish volunteers) were called to help defend the way on Witków [Wittichow], which was the only chance for retreating troops. The counter-attack of the battalion from the *'Frundsberg'* Division was a complete failure and forced the Walloons to escape complete defeat by retreating towards the swamps near Strzyżno [Stressen].[8]

Here we should hear Leon Degrelle, who describes the battle in colourful detail:

> As the night approached, there was drizzle in the air and a deep chill in our bones. Our company's small radio-station crackled. It was the general calling from Stargard. Their attack had failed, the joining of forces was impossible and the German tanks were supposed to fall back under the cover of the night. As for us, we were to quietly return to our morning positions in the evening.
>
> We barely managed to retreat through those muddy swamps, when I got an order to send one of my companies to our right flank, to Krussow, which was being defended only by a small group from *Volkssturm*.
>
> The town stretched along both sides of the Lindenberg-Stargard road. We were expecting the Russians to attack at any given moment, as they were quite emboldened by their successful defence yesterday.
>
> Our boys reached Krussow at exactly the same time the Soviet tanks did. They were pushed back to the other side of the River Ina. Their situation was singularly difficult. The company commander rallied their defences on the right bank but was able to do very little, since he had been sent there way too late. The village was important, though, and our officers did not yield easily.
>
> Without much noise, but with a heavy heart, the young company commander brought his men to order and phoned me to tell me of his plans.[9] Then he ran alone to Krussow and got himself killed by its walls.[10]

Although the situation in the sector was becoming critical, the Walloons fought bravely and by 5 February they managed to hold the road, making the attempt to transport supplies to Szczecin [Stettin] a success.[11] The areas where the fighting took place were engulfed in flames. The formerly tranquil towns and villages of the rural region, which used to be Western Pomerania, were rapidly

---

8   Ibid., p. 286.
9   Degrelle most likely means the CO of the 5th Company II/69 – *SS-Untersturmführer* Henri Rue, who was killed in Krussow on 12 February.
10   Degrelle, op. cit., p. 306.
11   de Bruyne, op. cit., p. 286.

25.   A local road-crossing through Kurcewo [Krussow]. (Tomasz Borowski)

26.   One of the households in Kurcewo [Krussow] remembering
the beginning of 1945. (Tomasz Borowski)

turning into dust from the destructive element. Many people despondently watched what was going on around them. Leon Degrelle, the Burgundian commander, shares his thoughts on the subject, trying to represent the cruelty of war, which could not be ignored:

> I was summoned to the corps's command post at two in the morning and I had to take my small Volkswagen through those raging ruins. The general had taken a villa in the upper part of Stargard. I received my orders and left the house through the garden. The city below me looked like a mighty ship set ablaze.
>
> Old quadrangular medieval towers stood severe and dark, a stark contrast with the fiery glow. They stood unmoved in the hurricane of flames, as if trying to send a call to the heavens, the last call of the ages of a civilisation in fiery agony. Those black towers on that red and gold backdrop was a sight to behold. They had never been so beautiful and never before had they borne such extraordinary witness. Miserable towers of Stargard, blackened masts of a burning ship that had carried the birthright of Christian Europe for five hundred years.[12]

---

12 Degrelle, op. cit., p. 311.

4

'Spring Solstice'

Due to the continuous push of Soviet armies, the German command decided on a risky aggressive action. The plan for this counter-attack was presented to Hitler by General Heinz Guderian.[1] The plan was to amass as many troops in as little time as possible and then to strike at the vulnerable wing of the 1st Belorussian Front.[2] The attack was to be preceded by the arrival of the elite 6th *SS Panzer* Army from the West. The *Fuhrer* rejected the proposal however, arguing that the army was more needed in Hungary.[3] Since the beginning of February, a concentration of forces in Western Pomerania had begun, in order to take part in an offensive code-named '*Sonnenwende*' [Spring Solstice]. Practically from the start, the troops deployed to the region were in heavy fighting with the advancing 61st Army. The Walloons are the perfect example. They barely managed to arrive in Pomerania when they had to bear the brunt of the battle with the Red Army near Kurcewo [Krussow] and the neighbouring settlements.

According to Guderian, the German troops were to achieve battle-readiness by 20 February, but due to Hitler's insistence on urgency, preparations for the attack were completed by the 14th. Despite insufficient preparation and having little chance of getting the proper fuel and ammo reserves, the date of the attack was set for 15 February 1945.[4] At this point it would be beneficial to recount the full complement of the *Kampfgruppe* if we are to truly appreciate the importance of Operation '*Sonnenwende*' to the *Wehrmacht* High Command. They deployed the most valiant *Waffen-SS* volunteer formations and elite *Wehrmacht* divisions. The 11th Army began the offensive in the following complement:[5]

---

1   At the time, Adolf Hitler was the supreme commander of the German Land Forces Command (*Oberkomando des Heeres* – *OKH*), which was directly responsible for the movements of German troops on the Eastern Front from the Baltic Sea to the Black Sea. Colonel General Guderian was the *OKH's* chief of staff. (ed.)

2   Brzeziński, Piotr, *Ocena Szans Operacji Zaczepnej o Kryptonimie Sonnenwende ...* , p. 3.

3   Michaelis, Rolf, *Nordland* (Warsaw, 2004), p. 57.

4   Brzeziński, op. cit., p. 5.

5   In most sources, the 11th Army appears as the *Wehrmacht* Field Army. The commander of the Army Group 'Vistula' however, called it the 11th *SS Panzer* Army. He wanted to impress Hitler by creating a new great formation mainly from *SS* troops. (ed.)

- 'Homlein' Corps with the 9th *Fallschirmjäger* Division between the Oder and the Miedwie Lake
- XXXIX *Panzer* Corps with the *Panzer* Division 'Holstein', the 10th *SS Panzer* Division *'Frundsberg'*, the *4th SS-Polizei Panzer-Grenadier Division* and the 28th *SS*-Volunteer Grenadier Division *'Wallonien'*, which is of most interest to us; they were deployed between the Miedwie Lake and the River Ina (it should be pointed out that at the start of *'Sonnenwende'* the Walloons weren't, in fact, under the command of the III *SS Panzer* Corps, as is mistakenly reported in some sources)
- III *SS Panzer* Corps (Germanic) with the 11th SS Volunteer *Panzergrenadier* Division *'Nordland'*, the *Kampfgruppe* from the 27th *SS*-Volunteer Grenadier Division *'Langemarck'*, the 23rd *SS-Panzergrenadier* Division *'Nederland'* and the 281st *Wehrmacht* Infantry Division stationed between the River Ina and the town of Recz [Reetz][6]
- 'Munzel' Corps with *'Führer Begleit Division'* and *'Fuhrer Grenadier Division'* which were to protect the wings towards Drawno [Neuwedell] and Drawsko Pomorskie [Drage]
- XX Army Corps with the *SS-Kampfgruppe* 'Schulz-Streeck', the 402nd *Wehrmacht* Division and the 5th *Jäger-Division* poised to push the attack towards Kalisz Pomorski [Kallies]
- the Special Operations 'von Tettau' Corps along with the *'Bärwald'* and *'Koslin'* Divisions and the 163rd *Wehrmacht* Infantry Division formed the army's left wing.[7]

All the soldiers were informed of the importance of their mission so that they would give their all.

In this strategic offensive operation, the Walloons were tasked with attacking the interchange near Lindenberg [Lipia Góra]. For their mission, the 7/II/69 was selected, under the command of *SS-Obersturmführer* Jacques Capelle. The orders received on 16 February 1945 were severe: hold the hill for 24 hours. This is Leon Degrelle's recollection of the first phase of the fighting:

> Lieutenant Capelle knew how to keep a cool head even in the most difficult
> of circumstances. He would send a short report over the radio every fifteen
> minutes. The Russian tanks cleverly kept out of range of the *panzerfausts*. They

---

6   The corps's mission was to free the surrounded Choszczno [Arnswalde]. (ed.)
7   Michaelis, op. cit., p. 60.

27.   The only photograph of *SS-Obersturmführer* Jacques Capelle –
here as a soldier of the '*Legion Wallonie*'. (Michel le Roy's collection)

fired on our positions metre after metre. We had a great many casualties. Still,
our comrades stood their ground fiercely and heroically.[8]

On the next day, the Soviets launched a devastating attack on the Walloon
positions. Capelle's men fell one by one but held out for 27 hours, three hours
longer than required. The price they had to pay for that success, however, was
high. *SS-Obersturmführer* Capelle and *SS-Untersturmführer* Jacques Poels were
both killed in action,[9] alongside 51 of the 110–120 men who manned their
positions.[10] The rest of them, using the cover of darkness, retreated from their
own lines through the marsh. Once again we quote Degrelle, who speaks of the
hell the 7th Company went through on the Lindenberg hill:

Our soldiers, stuck in that muddy spur, followed their orders bravely (...). The
wounded fought like everybody else, wanting rather to fall in battle than die
from a strike of a butt or some entrenching tool.

---

8   Degrelle, Leon, *Front Wschodni 1941-1945* (Międzyzdroje, 2002), p. 311.
9   de Bruyne, Eddy, Rikmenspoel, Mark, *For Rex and Belgium ...* (Solihull, 2004), p. 286.
10   Eddy de Bruyne's letter to the author from 13 April 2013.

28.   *SS-Untersturmführer* Jacques Poels: KIA on 17 February 1945 during the battle for Lipia Góra [Lindenberg]. (J.L. Roba's collection)

Capelle calmly reported over the radio of those last dying stages. The Soviet tanks were everywhere. The men, huddled in small groups, fought bitterly 'till the last moment. Finally, only the command post was left, like an island surrounded on all sides by howling murderous hordes.

When the hand-to-hand combat was over, Capelle, despite being grievously wounded, kept firing his gun. He stood tall and brave in the face of the Reds who were running at him. When they were only a metre and a half away, he put a bullet in his head.

Only four wounded soldiers, neck-deep in muddy water, witness the finale of that tragedy. When night fell, they crawled through the swamp. Two of them died in the mud of exhaustion. The other two, half-dead, were found by one of the patrols.[11]

Degrelle's words above – as well as those Eddy de Bruyne wrote in his book *For Rex and Belgium* – as they pertain to the death of *SS-Obersturmführer* Jacques Capelle – need some clarification, or an explanation at the very least.

By accident, the author was able to acquire a hand-written document by Rene Massot, a soldier in the 7th Company, who puts the aforementioned testimony into question. This is the entirety of the document:

Statement: Massot Rene (of Aubange)

---

11   Degrelle, op. cit., p. 316.

29. A view of a trench in which the Walloons were probably defending themselves from Soviet tanks. (Tomasz Borowski)

30. Marshes near Lipia Góra [Lindenberg]. (Tomasz Borowski)

Déclaration de Massot René (d'Aubange)

"Je faisais partie de la 7ᵉᵐ Compagnie à la défense du "Lindenberg". J'ai très bien connu le Lieutenant Capelle avec qui j'étais lié par une sincère amitié. Enssemble nous avons été "fait prisonnier" dans l'après-midi du 17 février 1945. Nous avons été conduits dans une cave avec quelques autres camarades. Dans la soirée du même Jour il fut comme officier séparé de notre groupe. Je ne l'ai plus revu depuis. Il est absolument faux qu'il ait été tué ou qu'il se soit suicidé au "Lindenberg". J'ai été conduit peu après dans une ville dont j'ai oublié le nom."

31.   Rene Massot's statement on the alleged death of
Jacques Capelle. (Michel le Roy's collection)

I was a soldier in the 7th Company and I fought at Lindenberg. I got to know Lieutenant Capelle very well and we became true friends. In the afternoon of 17 February 1945 we were both taken prisoner. They took us to a basement, where several of our mates were being held already. Because Capelle was an officer, on the evening of the same day he was separated from the rest of us. That was the last moment I ever saw him. It is preposterous to claim that he was killed or committed suicide on the Lindenberg hill. After that I was taken to a city, the name of which escapes me.[12]

Eddy de Bruyne is a Belgian historian and professor – and for years now he has been studying the collaboration of the French-speaking citizens of the Kingdom of Belgium with the Third Reich. When shown the aforementioned manuscript, he sheds a little more light on the matter at hand. In one of his letters to the author he explains that, when writing of Capelle's death, he based his account on the official chronicle of the Walloon Legion, a copy of which can be found, among other places, in the American Hoover Institute. The story is based on documents and memoirs by Walloon officers who had survived the war. Despite this seemingly indisputable proof, de Bruyne still had some reservations and he questioned the date of Capelle's death (17 February 1945) in one of his

---

12 Michel le Roy's archives, source unknown.

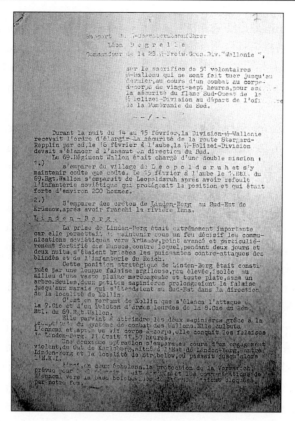

32.   A copy of a page from a report written on 18 February 1945 by *SS-Obersturmbannführer* Leon Degrelle on the fighting near Lipia Góra [Lindenberg]. (Michel le Roy's collection)

later publications. In 2010, in a French magazine about military history *Axe & Allies*, de Bruyne ultimately states that today practically no one knew for sure whether Capelle had been killed on the hill or taken prisoner and had died in captivity. Furthermore, de Bruyne concludes that the most proper term to describe Capelle's fate is 'MIA' – missing-in-action. As for Massot's statement, de Bruyne claims the document not to be an original, but a copy written by a third party. Its content, however, is unquestionable. After the war there was much discussion on the subject among veterans – some agreed with Degrelle's opinion, others argued against it.[13] It is doubtful, given the passage of time, that this episode will ever be truly resolved through indisputable evidence.

We can also only speculate on the reasons why Degrelle, when writing his memoirs, had depicted Capelle's alleged death in such heroic style. It is doubtful

---

13   Eddy de Bruyne's letter to the author from 16 April 2013.

he witnessed it himself; he rather based his story on the report of those soldiers who managed to reach their lines. Furthermore, we cannot exclude the possibility that Degrelle had intentionally embellished the facts in order to build a legend around the battle for Lindenberg, which was supposed to become the Walloon Thermopylae.

A very interesting view on this matter can be found in an article about the Lipia Góra, *Degrelle, Koniec Mitu ...* by historian Andrzej Szutowicz. In his article, Szutowicz impresses on just how difficult and hopeless it must have been for those soldiers to stand their ground and keep those defence positions. Having conducted field studies of the region, the author can only confirm Szutowicz's words. The hill overlooking the area must have been very hard to defend, indeed. The Walloons had to sit in hastily-dug foxholes and they also took trenches that may have been built by the Soviets earlier.[14]

As it was attacking the hill, the Red Army quickly realised that the defenders did not have heavy weaponry capable of successfully repelling the advancing tanks. Wanting to avoid casualties and loss of equipment, they left their armoured vehicles at a safe distance. Knowing the range of the *panzerfausts*, the only anti-tank weapons the Burgundians had at their disposal, the Soviets took positions outside of that range. Metre after metre, they fired on the points of resistance, successively destroying the entire line of defence. Hastily-built foxholes did not provide adequate protection from the shrapnel. Explosions and the thunder of guns mixed with screams of the wounded and dying Belgian soldiers. Every moment, some point of resistance was falling silent. Despite their great heart, they could not hold against the overpowering force of the enemy. Still, they chose to fight to the end, knowing how vital was the place they were defending. They also understood what would happen to them should they be taken captive. Even much earlier, as they fought on the Eastern Front, they witnessed the cruel treatment the prisoners from the *Waffen-SS* had suffered. Wounded soldiers stood arm-in-arm with their comrades. In those last moments of their short lives they perhaps thought of their loved ones left behind in their beloved Motherland. Numb to the pain, they left this world.[15] The Walloon sacrifice made a deep impression on the German command in the Pomerania.

On 27 February 1945, *Oberkommando der Wehrmacht* issued the following official announcement over the radio:

'On the Pomerania, the *Kampfgruppe* of the Volunteer Grenadier Division

---

14   Szutowicz, Andrzej, *Degrelle, Koniec Mitu, Czyli Tropem Walończyków i Ich Wodza*, p. 5.
15   Gerard Sopiński's letter to the author from 28 May 2013.

33.   The trenches mentioned in Andrzej Szutowicz's article. (Tomasz Borowski)

'*Wallonien*', under the command of *SS-Obersturmführer* Capelle, had fought and defended with unparalleled valour and fanatical fighting spirit'.[16]

Allegedly, on 1 March 1945, Capelle was posthumously nominated for the Knight's Cross of the Iron Cross. Unfortunately, no documents exist to confirm this theory.

Abel Delannoy remembers one of his fallen comrades as follows:

German tanks from the 10th *SS Panzer* Division '*Frundsberg*' attacked the little town near Arnswalde. They surrounded it and took control of it, wanting to be able to realise more ambitious goals in the counter-offensive. Our 7th Company from the 69th Regiment took position in Lindenberg – the lime hill – shielding them from attack. The Soviets advanced with their tanks to clench the Burgundians, who didn't have the support of heavy artillery. *Untersturmführer* Jacques Poels, the leader of the 1st Platoon, emerged from the trench armed with a *panzerfaust*, trying to stop an enemy tank. He was quickly targeted by the Reds, who fired on him with all their might, making

16   Szutowicz, op. cit., p. 2.

34.   Buildings in Strzebielewo [Streblow]. (Tomasz Borowski)

him jump, the gun still in his hand. He died instantly. Poor Poels got himself targeted even during training in Neweklau.[17] His *Junkerschaftsführer*,[18] Paul S., a Prussian if there ever was one, sent him to the roof of the building in the training grounds regularly. He would sit there, singing his lungs out, trying to reassure other *junkers*, as they crawled. Such is the image left in my memory. He was a kind and honest boy but he had that something many good Burgundians had! Lakaie, the CO of the battalion our 7th Company was a part of, asked one of the officers to replace Jacques. That officer turned out to be me. I was sad, leaving my platoon, which became a true family to me. When I arrived at Kremzow in the evening, the 7th Company was no longer.[19]

The defence of the interchange was one of the last episodes of Operation *'Sonnenwende'*. On 18 February, due to heavy fighting, the operation broke. Because of insufficient success and such heavy resistance from the Red Army,

---

17   An officers' school training *panzergrenadiers* in anti-tank defence, among others. The school was in Neweklau, near Prague.
18   Instructor.
19   Delannoy, Abel, *Confession d'un SS*, p. 40.

35.   The site of a church that used to stand there until 1945. The church
was built of Belgian blocks and brick. It was founded in 1833 by the road
to Strzebielewo [Streblow] from Stargard. (Tomasz Borowski)

Felix Steiner was forced to put a stop to the offensive on 20 February, which is
also considered the official end of *'Sonnenwende'*.[20] The retreating *'Nordland'* and
'Langemarck' Divisions were deployed along a new defence line by the River Ina,
while the *'Wallonien'* Division, along with the 322nd *Wehrmacht* Division, took
the front-line between Krępcewo and Strzyżno.

Leon Degrelle remembers the end of Operation *'Sonnenwende'* as follows:

> We returned to our old trenches. Behind our backs lay the demolished, burnt
> down, Stargard, like a forbidding ruined graveyard.
>
> The German offensive on 16 February 1945 on Landsberg, a parade of tanks,
> trucks and guns that we got to watch for four days, ended with the capture of
> only one humble village, Bralletin, and a couple of even smaller settlements.[21]

On 19 February 1945, the Walloon defence-line was reassigned under the

20   Brzeziński, op. cit., p. 17.
21   Degrelle, op. cit., p. 316.

command of the *'Nordland'* Division.

The Walloon positions at the time were the following:

- I/69 at Krępcewo [Kremzow]
- II/69 between Strzebielewo [Streblow] and Kurcewo [Krussow]
- I/70 in reserve for the III/24 from *'Nordland'* Division at Krępcewo [Kremzow]
- Command post in Radziszewo [Schneidersfelde]

By 1 March 1945, the Soviets made great progress and were closing in on the German lines around Stargard.[22]

Once again we call on Abel Delannoy for his recollection, as he was a participant of the events in question:

I reported in at the battalion's office in Kremzow. The administrative officer who signed me in practically jumped when he saw my service record.

'Aren't you, by chance, Louis Delannoy's son?'

For the record, lets us quickly note that the hour was late and the alcohol levels in the adjutant's bloodstream were high enough that he had forgotten about the military honours appropriate to my rank.

'Why yes!' I said. His response was to heartily slap me on the face, from all that joy I imagine! The adjutant's name was Robert Degand and he was from Borinage,[23] the same town as me. Furthermore in 1914-18, he served in the war with my father. That insubordinate slap cemented a friendship, which rewarded us both measurably in mutually beneficial exchanges. In the estate occupied by the Staff, there was a barn and Degand had kept all the cattle in Kremzow there, which was later successively turned into some juicy steaks.

'I'll trade you my alcohol rations for those steaks,' I told him. I was enabling his addiction, I know, but the food in my platoon improved greatly because of that.

My platoon joined me when one of the other battalions was crushed and we had to fill the hole in the line. We set our heavy machine guns in the crucial points around the town. Though the front was calm, I rode my men hard. I had them dig in regularly to await the hail of lead. I served as an example myself, having an entrenching tool always in my hand.

---

22 de Bruyne, op. cit., p. 286.
23 A region in Wallonia.

36.   The entrance to Krępcewo [Kremzow] from Stargard
Szczeciński [Stargard in Pommern]. (Tomasz Borowski)

Some German wandered off into the no-man's land that night. He failed to answer a guard's call, couldn't hear or understand it maybe, and he got himself foolishly killed with a German bullet. They lay him down in the corridor in a house. He was a big man, a peasant, sturdily built, like many all over German fronts. He would retain his stoic composure, whether in the face of an icy snow obstacle or in the middle of a Libyan storm. He wore civilian clothing under his uniform, because he wanted to cross the Russian lines. His luck had run out at the last moment! One of my stations is in a linesman's booth on the train-line Stargard-Arnswalde. I ordered the crew to reinforce the fortifications around the little house. It was high time: they shortened the front-line in preparation for our retreat to Stargard.

The Russians placed one anti-tank gun on the train-crossing in Kollin. That gun covered the entire line with fire, turning our defence into Swiss cheese. During the day my Burgundians couldn't so much as take a peak out of their foxholes. German pioneers jumping all over the tracks from place to place, riding a hand-car. The passengers set the arms of the lever between the seats. Its movement is transferred to the wheels by a cogged gear. Other men, from the engineering units, work like true moles digging more trenches, day and night.

Our Burgundians, who had no love for the infantry shovel, could learn a thing or two from those guys. We had them to thank for those trenches between Kremzow and our defence-line.[24]

In their positions before Kurcewo, the Walloons found themselves in a similar situation as in 1943/44 by the River Olszanka, during the Cherkassy Cauldron. Surrounded and alone, serving as the rearguard, stalling the enemy.[25] Degrelle confirms this:

> After the last offensive had failed, we were felt more alone than ever. Our line looked like a long fish-bone. The end of it was in Stargard, the head – in the villages Kremzow and Repplin in the south. The left flank (east) was confined between Ina's main current and the main road from Stargard to Schoneberg. The right flank (west) was limited by the lazy stream of Ina on one side and the village of Streblow and the Kolin settlement on the other.[26]

On 3 March, the bulk of the *'Wallonien'* Division found themselves near Witków [Wittichow].[27] Once again we quote Leon Degrelle:

> On Saturday, 3 March 1945, Stargard fell. Between that old Pomeranian city and our makeshift defence line lay only one big village called Wittichow and the crossroads in Klutzow, where a sugar factory stood.
>
> Fifteen days earlier the courtyards and halls of that factory were full of German tanks, which had come here for the offensive. Now, their emptiness was disturbed only by the sound of my Volkswagen's engine, as I drove through there, as the evolving situation demanded.[28]

Despite the pressure from the enemy and the risk of being cut off in the region, the Walloons had no choice but to stick to those few kilometres of the front they were tasked to defend.

On 4 March, the 'Derriks' Battalion was ambushed by the advancing enemy. They were saved from annihilation only by the immediate reaction from the cold-blooded commander of the 4th Company from the I/69, Bervaes.

24 Delannoy, op. cit., p. 40-41.
25 de Bruyne, op. cit., p. 286.
26 Degrelle, op. cit., p. 317.
27 de Bruyne, op. cit., p. 286.
28 Degrelle, op. cit., p. 320.

37.   A 15th century church in Strzebielewo [Streblow]. (Tomasz Borowski)

38.   Buildings in Strzebielewo [Streblow] situated by the road
to Krępcewo [Kremzow]. (Tomasz Borowski)

39.   *SS-Untersturmführer* Andre Regibeau (in the middle) - Commanding
Officer of the 1st Company in the I/69 – with his men during the
fighting near Kurcewo [Krussow]. (Michel le Roy's collection)

The 1st Company, under *SS-Untersturmführer* Andre Regibeau, was still
holding their forward positions between Strzyżno and Kurcewo. The 2nd and
4th Companies were entrenched in Strzyżno itself. In the morning, the German
defence-lines in the suburbs of Stargard were wiped out by the charging Russian
infantry and tanks. Around noon of the same day the tanks infiltrated the city.
Immediately, they engaged in fierce battle with the defenders. Meanwhile, the
1st Company had to face a powerful attack on Strzyżno, losing 48 soldiers (12
KIA, 36 WIA). *SS-Untersturmführer* Regibeau, though having been wounded
twice, refused to evacuate. Unwilling to leave his men, he continued the fight! *SS-
Oberscharführer* Mezetta and *SS-Oberscharführer* Fraikin later died from their
wounds.[29]

Degrelle tells the story of those tragic moments in his memoirs:

> The soul of the operation in Wittichow was a young officer in the Belgian Army,
> Major Hellebaut, already the chief of staff in our division. A brave soldier and
> an incurable idealist.

---

29   de Bruyne, op. cit., p. 287.

40.   A Walloon volunteer resting after battle near Kurcewo [Krussow]. (Eddy de Bruyne's collection)

The son and grandson of two Belgian generals – both of whom were ministers of war – he wore on his German uniform, next to the Iron Cross 1st Class, the Military Cross, which he had won by Izera in 1918.

Carried by his courage, the soldiers, who were fighting south of Wittichow, showed no fear and did not retreat, even though they had only eight kilometres to the walls of Stargard, which was under enemy fire since the late morning.

The rest of them were the last on the south and south-east line. They reinforced their positions and bravely held under attack from the east and south-west.

One by one, the companies stoically allowed themselves to be slaughtered. Second Lieutenant Paul Mezetta, the pillar of the Rexist Youth Organisation, died in mud, his belly ripped apart by shrapnel from a grenade. He was a singularly talented man, a poet and enthusiast. Even though he was terribly wounded in Caucasus, he was determined to return to the fight at all costs.[30]

One of the platoons, led by *SS-Hauptscharführer* Pierre Hancisse, was able

---

30 Degrelle, op. cit., p. 321.

41.   Paul Mezetta: fallen in
battle near Witków [Wittichow].
(Michel le Roy's collection)

to hold its position until 2:00 p.m., but that short-lived victory had cost them greatly. A little further away, the Russian infantry was trying to break through the swamps north of Witków, seriously threatening the Walloon positions. *SS-Obersturmführer* Henri Thyssen, together with a handful of volunteers, managed to keep them at bay for as long as the evening of 4 March. After that, the telephone line between command posts and the *'Wallonien's'* headquarters was broken. At around 4:00 p.m. Stargard Szczeciński was finally lost. A renewed attack on Strzyżno forced the 1st Company to leave the town.[31]

The Walloons were then ordered to hold their position between Witków and Strzyżno until 10:00 p.m. at all costs in order to allow the German forces – the artillery and an armoured train – to retreat.

The ever-present Abel Delannoy had been there as well:

> The Legionnaires, who had been able to escape the wave of Soviet attack, turned up on a different line, dug by those genius engineers – diggers. They definitely deserved the Order of the Golden Shovel, and made from solid gold, too! Things were calm again. An order was issued to hold the line until a set hour, the next stage of retreat. Will they attack? Will they not? They did not!

---

31   de Bruyne, op. cit., p. 287.

In silence we leave our trenches, heading towards the buildings in Wittichow. Our sergeant, Deprez – a golden man – him as well! – made us coffee and some pancakes to refresh us before the gruelling march ahead. On our right, Stargard-side, towns and villages are ablaze, as the Reds gain on us. Those evil fires get ahead of us. Onwards, that is backwards, our nightly marathon! We march with clenched teeth, without rest, our equipment spent and light and we can pass by the convoys slogging on the sandy roads.

'March, fight and hope like a true Legionnaire should!'

Before dawn we were in Seefeld. Having entered the closest house, dead tired, we fell asleep in our clothes, on beds and chairs.[32]

Another group of volunteers was able to halt the Soviet march until midnight – west of Stargard, on the way to Morzyczyno [Moritzfelde]. In the meantime, the Russians broke through the feeble defence-lines in many other places. Areas around Stargard came under fire from the north. At around 7:00 a.m. on 5 March, the aforementioned armoured train and the wounded soldiers left Witków on the last unoccupied road leading from Kluczewo to Kunowo. 'Derriks' Battalion evacuated from Strzyżno and retreated to Kluczewo, echelon by echelon. At around 10:00 p.m., the Walloons left Witków as well.[33]

SS-Obersturmführer Robert Buy, MD and a Catholic chaplain of the *'Wallonien'*, Father Gerard, by their repeated individual action, evacuated many soldiers who were badly wounded or otherwise unable to fight. At around 1:00 a.m. on 5 March, 'Derriks' Battalion, serving as the rearguard for the main force, was still holding the crossroads near Kluczewo. This allowed the last German troops to leave Stargard Szczeciński from the south side. On the same day, the 28th *SS*-Volunteer Grenadier Division *'Wallonien'* regrouped in Morzyczyno.[34]

They were in for another urgent mission: they were to return towards Grzędzice and take positions between Żarowo [Saarow] and Lubowo [Lubow]. Only 116 men from the I/69 and even less from the II/69 had reached Grzędzice in time. *SS-Sturmbannführer* Frans Hellebaut and *SS-Sturmbannführer* Jules Mathieu made their quarters in Bruckhausen, right next to *Oberstleutnant* Strelow, the commanding officer of the 322nd *Wehrmacht* Infantry Division, which was in charge of the region. Meanwhile, Leon Degrelle himself had arrived there and joined the command post of one of the *Wehrmacht* divisions in an old

---

32 Delannoy, op. cit., p. 44.
33 de Bruyne, op. cit., p. 287.
34 Ibid.

42.   Leon Degrelle among his soldiers. This photograph was surely taken
during the fighting in Western Pomerania. Proof of that is Degrelle's rank (he
was promoted to *SS-Obersturmbannführer* on 1 January 1945). Other details,
unfortunately, are unknown. (Jacques Grancher Publishing House archives)

former estate – Podlesie [Friedrichswalde].[35]

The German command wanted to rebuild the front-line around the region
in order to protect Szczecin and the mouth of the Oder. The units, who were to
perform the task, were already falling back for good and had lost most of their
combat strength earlier.

The Walloons were to stand in the way of the Russians advancing towards
Stargard Szczeciński from the north. Immediately after their arrival, both
Walloon battalions received the same order: take positions between Żarowo and
Lubow near the basin of Ina as soon as possible. Sadly, the 1st Battalion, once
in Grzędzice, could regroup only 119 men – and the other one, having left most
of its forces along the way, was even weaker. They also required at least a couple
of hours' rest, which is why both detachments reached the front-line only in the
evening.[36]

This was a critical moment, since the Burgundians had yet to form a coherent

---

35 Ibid.
36 Devresse, Roland, *Les Volontaires se la Jeunesse a la Legion Wallonie*, vol. 14, p. 55.

force capable of holding their line. Only individual actions by small strike groups, led by desperate commanders, were able to stall the onslaught of Russian forces – and that was only for just a short time. The Soviets had a great advantage of numbers and equipment alike.

Abel Delannoy, quite nonchalantly too, describes their retreat from Grzędzice:

> As we were sleeping, we were easy to find and but for one old Rexist, who came to wake us up, there'd be no more Burgundians in Seefeld. A Russian tank was firing on the exit from the town. Our morning workout now included a steady step, our speciality! We were gaining up on the refugees with their children and their bags, as they were running on foot. *'Gnadge Frauen'*,[37] we ask to light a candle for us by the statute of the Holy Mother, Protector of Outcasts of Egypt! All good Samaritans are now pushing the vehicles with children (*Rader mussen rollen fur den sieg ... und kinderwagen fur nachste Krieg!*[38]) and carrying luggage. During the day a staff officer met us at the crossroads, riding a courier's bike, and said we should go right, towards Saarow and Lubow, where the Burgundians were regrouping. They were trying to stop the advance of enemy tanks. We had been heading in the wrong direction all day. I think the battalion, regiment and division staff would be better served to place their officers and field MPs alongside the road on the way to Wittichow – Seefeld, so they could guide us better. These consecutive breakaways started to turn into 'run for your lives!'[39]

Military staff offices were still able to set command posts and issue orders, but they had to find soldiers to carry them out first.

The Russians were heading for Stargard Szczeciński. The enemy was met around Żarowo and crushed the feeble German forces. The situation was normalised again due to the intervention of the Walloon officers. They were also accompanied by a group of men who were to scout future positions.

At dawn, on 6 March, the Walloon 'Lakaie' Battalion, stationed in Lubowo, was ambushed and destroyed. Only a handful of legionnaires, lead by *SS-Hauptsturmführer* Henri Thyssen and *SS-Untersturmführer* Leon Gillis, was able to hold the line until they received artillery cover from 'Derriks' Battalion from the other side of the Ina. Soon, the Russians were near Żarowo. They cut into the

---

37 'Gracious lady' (German).
38 'The wheels must turn until victory comes ... and the baby strollers 'til the next war' – a sarcastic paraphrase of a German propagandist slogan.
39 Delannoy, op. cit., p. 44.

43. *SS-Sturmbannführer* Jules Mathieu – the CO of the 69th Regiment, '*Wallonien*' Division – during the Pomeranian Campaign. He is dressed in a *Wehrmacht* officer's uniform. (Jacques Grancher Publishing House archives)

Walloon positions like a knife through butter and forced the desperate defenders into a hasty retreat. *SS-Untersturmführer* Regibeau, who remained at his position until the end, like a captain willing to go down with his ship, was only able to save his own life by jumping into the icy waters of the Ina and swimming to the other side – dodging the rain of Soviet bullets by luck alone.[40] Leon Degrelle remembers the fierceness of the battle:

> My battalion from Lubow, having lost half their men, became pinned down on the right bank of the Ina, under Soviet tank fire. Falling back to Saarow, I had but a group of two hundred and fifty men. I did not have even a single tank to help in our resistance. (...) The field was covered with our wounded. With pain and horror we watched them being murdered: the Soviet infantry-men walking among tanks, bashing our poor comrades' heads in. One of them tried to wave a white hankie above his head to no avail. Just like all the others, he got his face smashed by those butchers.[41]

SS-Sturmbannführer Henri Derriks and his officers had to regroup in these

---

40 de Bruyne, op. cit., p. 288.
41 Degrelle, op. cit., p. 325.

difficult conditions. They were no longer able to defend the Bruckhausen region.

The terrain offered no cover so the *'Nordland'* and the 322nd *Wehrmacht* Infantry Divisions could not answer *SS-Sturmbannführer* Frans Hellebaut's desperate call for back-up. The Walloons' orders were harsh and clear: defend their positions at all costs! *SS-Sturmbannführer* Jules Mathieu's command post came under shrapnel shell fire and lost communication. Furthermore, *SS-Sturmbannführer* Henri Derriks got shot in the knee and was replaced by *SS-Obersturmführer* Marcel Bonniver. Remnants of the I/69, about 250 men, were still trying to halt the Soviet push. Also, their strife was for naught. At around 6:00 p.m., Hellebaut ordered Bonniver to leave their position under the cover of the night and move towards Podlesie, where the *'Wallonien'* Division had been engaging as the defensive rearguard for the *'Nordland'*.[42]

'Lakaie' Battalion in Lubowo

At this point, we should tell a little bit more about the fighting around Lubowo. The memories and analyses from eye-witnesses, as included in a study by *SS-Untersturmführer* Roland Devresse, a veteran of these battles, shed a new light on the previously unknown facts of these tragic events.

On 6 March 1945, at around 4:00 a.m., the 'Lakaie' Battalion took Lubowo on the right bank of the Ina and manned the best positions so as to successfully stop the first enemy assault, similarly as it had done in the past during the Pomeranian Campaign.

SS-Hauptsturmführer Leon Lakaie's men were still taking their defence posts around Lubowo when, at dawn around 6:30 a.m., the assault came. The violent and incredible concentration of enemy fire was accompanied by 15 tanks and a numerous infantry. The 'Lakaie' Battalion, already greatly weakened (they had lost a third of their complement, including nine officers, in the span of a month), were quickly defeated, practically cut into pieces. Lakaie could not evacuate the Ina's left bank since the rail-road bridge had just been destroyed by German sappers. The bridge's rubble was already floating down the river towards Roggowo [Roggow], taking the many wounded's hope for rescue right along with it. Among them was *SS-Untersturmführer* Desire Lecoq, the 6th Company of the II/69 CO, who died from his wounds.[43]

Predictably, the 'Lakaie' Battalion failed to stop the first enemy assault.

---

42 de Bruyne, op.cit., p. 288.
43 According to Jean Mabire, Lecoq was the commander of the 1st Company in the 1st Battalion of the 70th Regiment. Mabire gives Lecoq's date of death as the same as that of Roland Devresse.

44.   Two pages from SS-Untersturmführer Roland Devresse's military service book ['*Soldbuch*']. Devresse, among other postings, was a leader of the 3rd Platoon, 2nd Company in *Kampfgruppe 'Derriks'* during the tail-end of the fighting in the Rosówek [Neu-Rosow] region. (Eddy de Bruyne's collection)

What could those companies do? Weak, bled-out, having barely a platoon of men, exhausted by having to constantly stall the enemy and by gruelling retreat. The officers had no choice but to fight 'till the end and fall in battle. The list of casualties from the 2nd Battalion of the 69th Regiment *'Wallonien'* during those next battles was going to be a long one. The situation of Lubowo temporarily improved due to dedication and good organisation of a small strike group. We now give voice to a participant of these events – a leader of one of the platoons: *SS-Untersturmführer* GePe:[44]

> Twenty of the Flak/Pak Company's survivors had joined *SS-Obersturmfuhrers* Thyssen and Gillis around the railway embankment. They were trying to block the Russians from charging into the town. *SS-Hauptsturmführer* Derriks's battalion (1st Battalion of the 69th Regiment) was engaging the enemy on

---

44 The pseudonym is derived from the initials G.P. Out of respect for GePe's family, who did not wish for his full name to appear in official publications on the Walloon volunteers, the author chose to use that exact, official, alias.

the opposite bank, supporting them with suppressing fire and mortars. The effect was immediate: the German Pak-cannon, located by the north exit from Saarow, destroyed two tanks, as they emerged from behind Lubow buildings. *SS-Untersturmführer* Rudi Bal took a reserve support platoon and went to Roggow. He died trying to accomplish his mission.[45]

SS-Untersturmführer GePe was among those who went to help the 'Lakaie' Battalion. His recollection of events differs from the description made by his commander much later (after the action was over). It would be beneficial to cite a couple of excerpts from that description. They are in a form of a statement, which were also forwarded to other combatants: *SS-Hauptsturmführer* Jules Mathieu and *SS-Sturmbannführer* Frans Hellebaut. They clearly exemplify the obstacles one meets when trying to make an objective assessment of those battles. We should keep in mind, however, that every participant remembered them differently.

First, I shall remind you briefly that 'Lakaie' Battalion's strength was not adequately assessed, seeing as how they were ordered to defend Lubow with the feeble forces and resources at their disposal. Two pseudo-companies, commanded by young Walloon officers who had just arrived! No military staff offices to speak of. Are your eyes deceiving you? None. With that in mind, *SS-Sturmbannführer* Hellebaut chose a couple of the officers who had arrived at Wittichow, heading for Saarow, to take the command post after *SS-Hauptsturmführer* Derriks. The were to accompany Hellebaut with a large platoon created from *SS-Untersturmführer* Rudi Bal's company.

This supportive action was to take place under the cover of the night, behind the rail-road bridge, that connected the two banks of the Ina and Saarow with Lubow. The next morning, on 6 March 1945, when the battle had just begun, the German sappers blew the bridge up, rather hastily, according to Hellebaut. I do not share his opinion on the subject.

The participants of the excursion: Bal and his men, *SS-Hauptsturmführer* Henri Thyssen, *SS-Obersturmführer* Gillis and myself.[46]

SS-Untersturmführer GePe proceeds to describe the battle. His version is similar to that of *SS-Hauptsturmführer* Leon Lakaie since GePe was assigned as his 'bodyguard'. They fought side by side and therefore it is not hard to imagine

---

45 Devresse, op. cit., p. 56.
46 Ibid.

45.   This photograph depicts two brothers: GePe on the left and Pierre on the right. Between the two we can see Leon Degrelle's daughter. Pierre was killed in action in the Cherkassy Cauldron. GePe was a Commanding Officer in Pomerania as a leader of two different platoons. (Charles Verpoorten's collection)

that this was the reason why GePe could not help but to defend Lakaie from criticism after the battle for Lubowo was over.

> On 6 March the entire Lubow came under violent bombarding, promising a regular infantry assault. Together with Henri Thyssen and Leon Gillis, I witnessed a telephone conversation between our commanders: Lakaie and Hellebaut. Lakaie was demanding reinforcements and Hellebaut was invariably saying: 'I don't have them, hold on, hold on. Take the tanks with bayonets, if you have to!'[47]

Meanwhile, the pressure on the second battalion's command is reaching its peak. *SS-Obersturmführer* Gillis is pissed and joins his men in the strife. *SS-Hauptsturmführer* Thyssen and *SS-Untersturmführer* GePe are trying to convince *SS-Hauptsturmführer* Lakaie to leave his battle station and join the defence, which would make it easier to lead.

Thyssen said he wanted to go and see what was up with Gillis because he was

---

47 Ibid.

worried about him. He begged me not to leave Captain Lakaie. The town consisted of two rows of houses standing at either side of the main road, in a fashion common to most small settlements in the Pomerania and in Prussia. At the front – Bal, Gillis and Thyssen. On the other side, from the Ina, a hundred and fifty metres' worth of meadow, the terrain was exposed. Its resistance ended quickly, but I managed to renew it ...

The centre of the town, where I hunkered down with Lakaie, was all quiet. We placed the machine guns in a good position, between two hills surrounding a garden. This allowed us to control the road on one side and block the enemy's approach from the Ina on the other.

I clearly remember as we lay there. Lakaie was out of sorts because he wasn't used to hand-to-hand combat. He had just arrived from a German POW camp, Oflag, and before that, at Stargard, he had been stationed at a command post, at the rear. I wasn't concerned too much, 'cause I knew we all had our better or worse moments, especially since I felt very well – I was calm and confident.[48]

Next, the two Walloon officers went on a scouting mission, searching for positions manned by their countrymen. According to Roland Devresse, *SS-Untersturmführer* GePe often made decisions on his own, given his CO's – *SS-Hauptsturmführer* Lakaie – lack of combat experience.

I went to take a look around. A hundred and fifty metres of meadow, then the river and nobody in sight. Just half an hour ago, I met a few survivors from the two companies commanded by our young officers, as they were retreating on their own. I yelled at them: 'Desertion, court martial!' and drew my revolver. Embarrassed, they made a half-turn and returned to their battle stations. Soon however, they started to retreat again, keeping up the pretence of order in this obvious mess.[49]

SS-Untersturmführer GePe reported to *SS-Hauptsturmführer* Lakaie on the situation. Lakaie was very upset but he still moved towards the church, wanting to continue the reconnaissance of the town. GePe disagreed with him but still had to follow. Suddenly, a Soviet T-34 tank appeared out of nowhere. The Walloons didn't have any *panzerfausts* to defend themselves with, so their situation was critical. Far away, by the railway embankment, they saw some soldiers who were

---

48 Ibid., p. 58.
49 Ibid.

46.　Walloon volunteers in a Pomeranian village. From left: *SS-Obersturmführer* George Suain (Platoon Leader in the 70th Regiment of the '*Wallonien*' Division), *SS-Obersturmführer* Leon Gillis (Company Commander in *Kampfgruppe 'Derriks'*), *SS-Obersturmführer* Desire Lecoq (CO in the 1st Company of the 70th Regiment – fallen on 6 March 1945 in Lubowo [Lubow]), *SS-Oberscharführer* van Isschot and *SS-Sturmmann* Collard. (J.L. Roba's collection)

gesturing and nervously waving at the two officers to run to them quickly.

> From their vantage point, they had a good view of the situation. Ambushed by the enemy, who had the advantage of numbers and equipment and tanks, they were huddled behind the first available cover, which was the railway embankment, located a hundred metres from the town.
>
> Lakaie and I lunged forward, like two gazelles. After thirty metres, however, Lakaie's gazelle turned into an exhausted snail. I had to wait for him and drag him by the arm the rest of the way. Thyssen, Gillis, Bal and the others gave us a beautiful covering fire. The Russians weren't as motivated (what did they need a couple of such pitiful individuals for, anyway?). The T-34 was firing, too. Finally, we reached our 'saviours', who later said that for a moment they

thought we were as good as taken.[50]

It became impossible to defend Lubowo. The group of Walloon officers made the only possible and reasonable choice. 'There was no other way. We had to fall back to the closest neighbouring town, which was Roggow, in this case. We decided to approach the river behind the embankment's cover, and then follow it all the way to Roggow. We split into small five-man groups, spread ten to fifteen centimetres apart.'[51] SS-Sturmbannführer Frans Hellebaut, one of 'Wallonien's' staff officers, stated: 'The retreat goes badly, SS-Untersturmführer Rudi Bal's platoon was annihilated ... '.[52] GePe contradicts these words.

> I present my thoughts. You will agree with me, I have no doubt. Clenching our fists, we both have to face the situation with cold blood. I also ask you to make your own assessment. It was decided then that Bal and a few of his men (four or five) would retreat last. Gillis and I went just before them. After our friends had retreated earlier, we went back to the railway embankment to fire on Lubow, particularly on that T-34. We had no choice but to move towards its striking distance. The trick was to distract the enemy so that our men could safely cover as long a distance as possible.[53]

GePe's recollection clearly indicates that the retreat from Lubowo seemed as organised as the resources at their disposal allowed. They were greatly insufficient but what could these soldiers do, when they were facing tanks, armed only with infantry weapons? We now give the floor to GePe, once again:

> When our turn came, I moved out with a handful of men. Nobody got shot, so far. Bal was some two metres behind us. All was going well, except that no one was left to cover our rear. Some one hundred and fifty metres behind us, the T-34 started firing. We were already used to it, so we didn't panic. After a while it was shooting again. It had replenished its ammo, no doubt. Luckily, the Soviet bombardier had really bad aim. He kept missing us. After a moment though, he readjusted his measurements and fired again, hitting the ground right behind us. Very, very close. Each time – I don't think I have to spell this

---

50 Ibid., p. 59.
51 Ibid., p. 60.
52 Ibid.
53 Ibid., p. 61.

47.   *SS-Untersturmführer* Rudi
Bal. (Eddy de Bruyne's collection)

out – we would lunge and flatten ourselves on the ground in one jump. Leon Lakaie and I turned back and we saw that Rudi Bal took a direct hit and was fatally wounded. So were the five or six men he had with him. Everything there was destroyed. Body parts were flying all around.[54]

As we see, things were not as simple out there, in the field. The point of view of a common soldier or a line officer would differ, more or less, from the concepts of the staff command. What more could these men do, when confronting such harsh reality? They fought desperately in a battle that seemed lost from the start.

We could have gotten to Roggow without casualties. Unfortunately, we were a couple of minutes short, just enough to learn that Regibeau had joined us (Gillis and me). He was soaking wet, having emerged from the river moments before. He had jumped into the water with the last of his ammo, hunted by the Russians all the way to Saarow.[55] Untersturmführer Desire Lecoq came, I don't know where from, and he was shot. He had been fired at by German artillery, who must've gotten some crazy, senseless orders. He died from blood loss[56] in a

---

54 Ibid.
55 This incident is also mentioned in Leon Degrelle's *Front Wschodni 1941–45.*
56 Lecoq's death had been mentioned already, but because it is an integral part of the matter at hand, the

German hospital in Roggow.[57]

We should remember that a four-unit Wehrmacht artillery battery was stationed in the west part of the town. The battery was supporting Henri Derriks's men in Saarow for a moment. Aiming towards Lubow, they wrongly set their sights on Roggow and consequently fired on our positions by mistake. We told them about it and with a proper reprimand too, obviously, because Lecoq's tragedy was still fresh in our memory.

Through a liaison officer, the battery commander asked us to leave the town and join them. We had to go through a small forest, only a hundred metres deep, just off the west side of the town. We did as much. Then he told us about his situation. Isolated, cut off from his own unit or other German formations, he asked our infantry to secure his battery for as long as he had ammo.

We agreed. With madness, worthy of Burgundians, we formed a defensive line on that plain, completely exposed behind the forest overlooking it. Our positions were uncomfortable, to say the least, and they were in direct contradiction with every rule on using the terrain in the book. In the meantime, the Russians in the forest targeted us and we heard the first salvoes. Their sharpshooters' bullets reaches us, officers huddled on less than fifty square metres of ground. Loneliness and mounting pressure made themselves known. I crawled towards the artillery-men and told them to aim directly where we tell them, exactly where the signal was coming from. The commanding officer agreed and, after two shots, all was quiet again.

We allowed the battery to collect itself, prepare everything and move out to find its unit.[58]

This action is not well known and the above fragment of GePe's recollection allows the uninitiated reader to learn of its atmosphere, even if these memories tend to be a little too detailed at times. In any case, they surely enrich the entire story. GePe firmly believes the last defenders of Lubowo deserve respect for what they did. The manner of their retreat and their support of the artillery battery should be appreciated. Their contribution to the saving of a great many human beings was unprecedented.

And so we soon moved out to Poczernin [Putzerlin], where the front was still

---

author had decided to recount it once again.

57 Devresse, op. cit., p. 62.
58 Ibid.

48.   *SS-Sturmbannführer* Frans Hellebaut. (*Axe & Allies* Magazine)

holding, thank God. A short while later we arrived at the command post, where *Sturmbannführer* Hellebaut was making sure the positioning of Walloon units was proceeding in a calm and orderly fashion.[59]

Again, we shall hear from *SS-Sturmbannführer* Frans Hellebaut, who confirmed his negative opinion on Leon Lakaie, without belittling the merits of the defenders from Lubowo. In a letter to GePe, Hellebaut declared:

> Still, despite everything and at the risk of disappointing you, I firmly believe it would not be beneficial to put too much emphasis on that episode in Lubow in light of the entire Pomeranian campaign. The episode had no bearing on the Burgundians' involvement. It may even suggest, frankly speaking, that the soldiers fell victim to their own commander, who was in over his head.[60]

Hellebaut admits it was hard to accuse his good friend and a fellow prisoner in an oflag, who enthusiastically had enlisted in the Walloon Legion with him. However, he reproaches him for his style – not military enough – and for being too lenient on his subordinates. This assessment is confirmed in another excerpt

---

59   Ibid.
60   Ibid., p. 63.

from his correspondence:

> Unfortunately, he was too good to his men but only because he treated Burgundians as if they were his own children. Even in Streblow I had to point out to him that his men weren't vigilant enough and that his way of commanding the battalion was too casual. That was not the best way to lead the defence and the entire platoon paid dearly for it.[61]

Regarding Lubowo, Hellebaut mainly points out that the units were positioned badly, which was why the battalion was doomed to fail from the start.

> The battalion's numbers barely reached a hundred and fifty men because Lakaie allowed most of them to scatter towards Altdamm. The 2nd Battalion could've taken the men from the 322nd Grenadier Division in twenty four hours earlier if Lakaie had not allowed his men to rest in Saarow all day. How were the Burgundians supposed to fight in Lubow at dawn on 6 March, when they had just barely arrived, still in complete darkness, without scouting the terrain and with no tactical directions, which were their commanding officer's duty to provide?[62]

These criticisms seem appropriate at this point; we should remember however that the Walloons were retreating in complete chaos. This is the reason why *SS-Hauptsturmführer* Leon Lakaie cannot bear the sole responsibility for the stray units. His cadre was increasingly weak, because the fighting south of Stargard Szczeciński had cost him his best officers. It would be beneficial to cite GePe's comments, who seems to be very close to the truth:

> In reality, Lakaie only had those officers Henri Derriks had discarded earlier.[63] Derriks keeps taking the best men, while 'diluting' the rest of the unit's cadre.[64]

After the war, Frans Hellebaut remembers the matter a little differently, comparing Leon Lakaie's 2nd Battalion's activities to the 1st Battalion under Henri Derriks.

---

61 Ibid.
62 Ibid., p. 64.
63 *Kampfgruppe* 'Derriks' was treated as an elite formation comprised of only the best soldiers from the Division *'Wallonien'*.
64 Devresse, op. cit., p. 64.

49.   *SS-Untersturmführer* GePe.
(Michel le Roy's collection)

Hellebaut's opinion, however, may seem hurtful to the former:

> To reinforce Lubow, I sent everything I still had, allowing the 2nd Battalion to
> slowly and steadily fall back, just as Derriks's battalion was doing during the
> day. He was facing a much larger enemy force (twenty eight combat-ready tanks
> were waiting at Saarow's northern turnpike, ever since the afternoon). So this
> wasn't that impossible, considering Thyssen, Gillis and Bal managed it in time
> and with only but a handful of men. They were the ones who proved their cold
> blood and quick understanding of the mission at hand.[65]

Additionally, *SS-Sturmbannführer* Hellebaut had to listen to many harsh
words from the German side, and the commanders of the neighbouring sectors
did not spare him their insults. It should be, therefore, understandable that he
did not remember these particular conflicts fondly.

At this point, it would be worth it to reach for a certain proof that sheds
a whole new light on the Lubowo [Lubow] matter and furthers the discussion.
The commanding officer of the 69th Regiment of the *'Wallonien'* Division, *SS-
Hauptsturmführer* Jules Mathieu, had his own views on the situation in a larger

---

65 Ibid.

perspective:

> At the start, I would like to strongly emphasise that the optics of any given operation are depending on the particular units in question. These differences come from different points of view. A division's commander has his perspective and a regiment's commander has his, including a broader picture. We can continue this reasoning through battalions, companies, platoons, etc. The details extend giving place to the totality of higher levels where a retreat is always a retreat, no matter if it was well conducted or not.[66]

This opinion may be regarded as a realistic assessment of the situation by a man, who came up through the ranks: from platoon leader to commander of a regiment.[67]

> As I am writing these words, the 2nd Battalion's retreat is not going well. And this is not to say anything against the 2nd Battalion 'Lakaie'. The Germans had given up earlier, even before he did. Derriks (1st Battalion's CO) had to do it a little later. Our respective commands were forced to criticise like everybody else. At the highest levels the dry account of the retreat makes us realise that this particular way of seeing things is inhumane. It can't be helped, though. The orders come from up top and they are always the same: to hold the line no matter what, no matter if the group is armed only with sticks.[68]

According to Jules Mathieu, everybody was doomed to play their role in these scenarios – already predetermined to fail. It was the commanders' duty to reassure their men and keep them in the fight. They could only hope their actions would help the lower ranks survive.

> I'm aware Major Hellebaut had lectured Lakaie on the weakness of his leadership – yet another typical squabble between career soldiers. I don't know if anyone would be able to defend themselves if a couple of earlier episodes came under scrutiny. (...)
>
> Now, after some time had passed, a sentimental aspect seems to come to the forefront. I like Leon Lakaie very much. But if I were to become a military

---

66 Ibid., p. 65.
67 Jules Mathieu means Frans Hellebaut, whom he quotes.
68 Devresse, op. cit., p. 65.

Leon Degrelle im Schützengraben

an der Front in Pommern. Der Kommandeur der wallonischen ᛋᛋ-Freiwilligen
verteilt Zigaretten unter seine Männer

ᛋᛋ-PK-Aufn. Niquille (Sch)   J 28764   Presse-Hoffmann

50.   In March and April 1945, Degrelle was rarely seen at the front-line; his
visits may be considered sporadic. Here is an official propaganda photograph
showing him in the trenches among his soldiers. (Michel le Roy's collection)

man again, as I had been in the past, when I was familiar with the awful state of
our battalion, I'm sure I would repeat after Major Hellebaut: 'We have to hold,
take those tanks with bayonets, if need be!' And, while giving such an order, I
would try to hide my own despair.[69]

After heavy fighting around Lubowo, the Walloons fell back to Wielgowo
[Augustenwalde]. This time it was the end. What was left of the Walloon
Kampfgruppe no longer had any coherence left – and they were not an exception
among the many units defending this particular area. Only a few pitiful German
units were still trying to stop the Russians, who were advancing towards Dąbie
[Altdamm] in order to take Szczecin, a great Baltic port already. In Roland
Devresse's memoirs we read:

Around two hundred and fifty Walloon fighters, who were still alive, arrived

69 Ibid.

in Augustenwalde in the meantime. They turned up at dawn, in small groups, exhausted by a dangerous fifteen kilometres' march. At night they crossed the Munsterberg forest, while still fighting to stall the enemy. They found Degrelle, as well as a couple hundred of his friends, who had made their quarters in small houses of the garden district. They were the survivors of the Flemish, German and Scandinavian units who managed to get out of their positions covered by a wave of Russian tanks.[70]

Having fought for many days, under extreme stress, these exhausted men were desperate for the peace and quiet of Wielgowo. This delicate idyll was shattered, however, when the Russian counter-attack came soon thereafter. Roland Devresse's recollection:

Sadly, the spell was broken around 1 PM, when a couple of enemy tanks opened fire, aiming at the openings of the forests nearby. Under cover of the German anti-tank defence, which brought down two T-34s, our men quickly fell back to safer positions – but it was only a scouting patrol! Few of them even understood what had happened. They could hear the echo of heavy fighting, from Rosengarten. The German command evacuated hastily ... It didn't take much to send those worn-down men, already at their breaking point, into panic. Frans Hellebaut and the others tried to keep things under control, but their efforts were in vain. Even Degrelle himself drove some of the Walloons to Dąbie in his own car.[71]

Here is Leon Degrelle's description of this event:

I got to Wielgowo [Augustenwalde] at 10 AM. This large village was located at the north-west end of the forest, about twelve kilometres east of Stettin. The place seemed well covered by the mass of trees and so the corps offices had been moved here the previous evening. I went to the general. The chief of staff, *SS-Obersturmbannführer* von Bockelberg, continuously on his phone, was giving me desperate signs. As the reports were coming in, he kept tapping the map: 'Twenty tanks here! Fifteen tanks here! Thirty tanks here!' He wiped his forehead and after a moment he told me, 'They are everywhere, they are coming from everywhere.'

70 Ibid., p. 68.
71 Ibid.

51.   Another photograph in the propaganda style. It was taken in the
1st Company's (*Kampfgruppe 'Derriks'*) operations area. First on the
left: *SS-Untersturmführer* Jacques Leroy. (J.L. Roba's collection)

Well, since those times on the Dnieper we had went through many such days,
when all was about to fail.

The corps trucks were there, so there was no catastrophe. Finally, I managed
to gather some of my men, including my officers, in the village. All around, pots
filled with chicken were bubbling over fires, in accordance with the best army
traditions. We practically threw ourselves at them to get a taste.

A couple of bullets knocked at the façade of the house. Another one,
slightly less discreetly, punched through the window and dug into the wall.
'They're killing chickens,' said Major Hellebaut matter-of-factly. Thirty, forty
more bullets flew in. 'I think they are killing a lot of chickens,' I allowed myself
to make a small point. Everybody went back to eating. This time a slew of shells
shook the entire building. 'They are even killing chickens with tanks,' I pointed
out more firmly. I passed my neighbour a plate with some tasty fruit from a jar

we found in the basement of the absent owner.[72]

This humorous picture quickly turned into a catastrophe. In a mess that was difficult to describe, the command staff were getting their things together. The Walloons did so as well. They were not the only ones to get out of places that started to heat up really fast.

---

72 Degrelle, op. cit., p. 329.

5

The Regrouping and the Crossing of the Oder

The Walloons started to regroup south of Dąbie [Altdamm]. The officers were trying to rebuild, platoon after platoon, company after company. Jean Mabire, a French writer and one of the greatest experts on the subject, wrote a book *Division de Choc Wallonie, Lutte a Mort en Pomeranie* where he describes the solemn atmosphere of those last days of the Pomeranian Campaign:[1]

There was one thing which kept everybody up: locate the Oder and get to it. But in order to cross the river, they first had to go through Altdamm. While passing by the town, Lieutenant Colonel Degrelle walked down the line of barbed wire fence of the prison camp. These were not enemy soldiers, cooped up in open space, in snow and mud, guarded by sentries. These were Germans! Haphazardly gathered up by the military field police, they were considered fugitives, if not deserters. They had to face some improvised court martial so it was difficult to predict the outcome. Bodies were swinging on the bridges of Oder, wooden tablets on their chests, saying *Feigling*.[2] It was not an accusation that could be forgiven in a country in agony, whose troops are still retreating in an orderly fashion and whose escape west creates fear in the civilian populations.

Chief! Chief! There were a couple of dozen of Walloon soldiers among those prisoners. More or less willingly, they were cut off from their unit, swept up by the wave of retreat. Small-time clever-clogs stood next to some true scum, who stood next to those who were simply pushed past their breaking point. There were also kids there, fifteen or sixteen years old from the youth units of the Walloon Legion, thrust into the terrible firestorm of war, holding on through months of endless battle.

Chief! Chief! They recognised him and now they think he is the only one

---

1　This book is based on the memories of many Walloon veterans who had fought in Pomerania and with whom Jean Mabire was in direct or postal contact. The publication has the form of a dramatised novel.
2　Coward.

52.   SS-Untersturmführer Mathieu de Coster (first on the right) with
his comrades during training. (Michel le Roy's collection)

who can get them out of this mess. They knew well what waited for them. The Walloon *Volksführer* was deeply moved by the plight of his countrymen. Not everybody has what it takes to be a hero. He tried to intercede on their behalf with the German command and managed to get a release for those of the Burgundians who made a mistake but were willing to return to their comrades in the division. They joined the regrouping near Altdamm subsequently.[3]

Even though Degrelle always paid much attention to the smallest details and gestures, he mentions nothing of this episode in his book *Eastern Front 1941–45*. Maybe he wanted to show humility, to downplay his role in the matter or maybe he just wanted to tell only the story of some of the feats his soldiers had performed, the feats which were more commendable. Whichever the case may be, Jean Mabire was told this story by many witnesses who hoped that their former chief's more human side would not be forgotten as time goes by.

Interestingly, this incident is not mentioned in any written documents of the *'Wallonien'* Division. We can only speculate that simply nobody wanted to

---

3   Mabire, Jean, *Division de Choc Wallonie, Lutte á Mort en Poméranie* (ed. Jacques Grancher, 1996), p. 199.

talk about it. Degrelle's appearance, when he came to save his people from that quagmire, can be seen as a minor detail, since the reverse situation would have been received as an incredible cowardice on his part![4]

This is how the crossing of the Oder is remembered by Mathieu de Coster, a former commander of the 2nd Company in *Kampfgruppe 'Derriks'*:

> We crossed the Oder. We went in small groups, new orders steadily coming in. A couple of German gendarmes were minding those who were crossing the river. I still had about forty men in my company. We crossed in threes in the column. We kept our march in order so we didn't raise any eyebrows. Without doubt we were the last ones of the *SS 'Wallonien'* who managed to get to the other side.[5]

4   Devresse, Roland, *Les Volontaires se la Jeunesse a la Legion Wallonie*, vol. 14, p. 70.
5   Ibid., p. 71.

6

Altdamm – Silence
before the Storm

Despite their subsequent failings, the III *SS Panzer* Corps (Germanic), which had been moved from the 11th Army to the 3rd *Panzer* Army, was still able to keep relative coherence. Due to some skilful stalling tactics, it was possible to keep the front from a complete breakdown. The right flank, holding the line near Miedwie Lake [Madu], was keeping up its defence thanks to the great efforts of the 281st *Wehrmacht* Infantry Division, commanded by the General Ottner, and two Walloon battalions. The left flank was being supported by the 10th *SS Panzer* Division 'Frundsberg', whose reserves had arrived from Gryfice [Greifenhagen].

In the meantime, the Deputy Supreme Commander Marshal Georgy Konstantinovich Zhukov[1] ordered his 61st Army to take Dąbie[2] [Altdamm] by bracketing the German forces and cutting off the retreating III *SS Panzer* Corps (Germanic), which was supposed to result in its destruction.[3] This time the 28th *SS*-Volunteer Grenadier Division 'Wallonien', which had worked closely with the aforementioned corps in earlier battles, had been formally incorporated into it.[4]

Since the beginning of the campaign in Western Pomerania, the Walloons had lost about 325 men – 125 of whom (including seven officers) were killed in action and 200 had been wounded. The unit had lost 11 anti-tank and/or anti-aircraft cannons. The better part of their heavy equipment had been broken. A lot of their light weaponry and infantry equipment had been lost during the heavy fighting. The division's car pool had been reduced to but a few vehicles. Hundreds of soldiers, cut off from their comrades, were scattered all over the area of the fighting during difficult nightly retreating manoeuvres. A couple of days'

---

1   The fighting of the right (north) wing of the 1st Belorussian Front are considered to be a part of the Pomeranian operation. Also, from November 1944, Marshal Zhukov was the direct commanding officer for that entire front. (ed.)

2   Currently a district of Szczecin.

3   de Bruyne, Eddy, Rikmenspoel, Mark, *For Rex and Belgium* ... (Solihull, 2004), p. 289.

4   <http://www.lexikon-der-wehrmacht.de/Gliederungen/GrenadierdivisionenSS/28GDSS.html> [time of access: 17/07/2013].

rest was absolutely necessary to return the formation to combat-readiness. The *'Wallonien'* Division, now reduced to the numbers of a strike group, was deployed to Gumieńce [Scheune],[5] behind the Oder's western banks, where the support and reserve Walloon troops were gathered to regain their strength and efficiency.[6]

Despite a fiery and passionate speech of the Walloons' formal and spiritual leader, Leon Degrelle, most of the survivors were spent and aware that they had done everything they could, and their morale was gone. The Legion's volunteers realised that further involvement and sacrifice might be completely useless.

In his later recollection, Degrelle explains his decisions on the matter:

> I was given a week to reorganise my crippled troops with the reinforcements, which had arrived at the Stettin railway station that morning.
>
> I wanted to keep only the toughest. I gathered them all, thanked them for their amazing service. In no uncertain terms I told them of the situation and of the harsh battles still ahead. 'Everybody may choose if they want to get back into the fray or hang back at the rear. Everybody had enlisted in the Legion voluntarily. No hope is left: I will accept your blood only if it is shed willingly. Nobody will be able to say that there was even one Walloon, who had fallen in our last fight against his will.'
>
> Eighty men chose not to return to the fight. I treated them with as much kindness as before. After all, I wasn't a slave overlord. Besides, most of these boys were at the end of their ropes. I sent them thirty kilometres to the north-west of Oder. I ordered that they were to be taken care of and well-fed.[7]

Only the most determined *SS* were still prepared to continue the fight. Degrelle describes their commander:

> The commander of the battalion of the 'toughest' was Major Derriks, a typical colonialist, who came here from the virgin woods of Congo, straight into the snowy steppes, always a crooked kepi on his head. He was a very brave soldier, a 'Captain Conan' type,[8] who came through Katanga.[9] He had the heart of a

---

5   Currently a district of Szczecin.

6   de Bruyne, Rikmenspoel, op. cit., p. 290.

7   Degrelle, Leon, *Front Wschodni 1941-1945* (Międzyzdroje, 2002), p. 330-331.

8   Degrelle means the hero of a French novel of the same title by Roger Vercel. The novel was published in 1934 and it tells the story of a young hero, Captain Conan, leading a group of courageous and gallant soldiers fighting in the Balkans in 1918 during the First World War.

9   A part of the Belgian colony in Africa, the Belgian Congo, which became famous for the bloody secession attempts in the 1960s of the 20th century. (ed.)

53.   *SS-Sturmbannführer* Henri Derriks is pictured here in a Legionnaire's uniform – prior to the formation's reassignment to the *Waffen-SS*. (Michel le Roy's collection)

child and he offered his loyalty with honesty and sincerity, which would bring tears to his eyes immediately.[10]

On 12 March 1945 *SS-Sturmbannführer* Henri Derriks, referred to by his men as 'Boss', after treating his wounds, returned to his troops and gave a speech – the last words of which were: 'Those who still believe and have the courage, step to the fore!' Twenty-three officers and 625 soldiers did as much ...

And so the battalion was rebuilding, breathing life into the Walloon Legion's ideals once again. Among those who willingly chose to stay, morale became quite singular. Life was going on as usual in their new quarters: silence before the heavy fighting soon to come. People eat, drink and sleep comfortably. The evil of the past days forgotten!

The volunteers formed a new unit, named after its commanding officer, *SS-Kampfgruppe 'Derriks'*. Equipment at their disposal:

- 400 rifles Karabiner 98k. Mauser
- 150 assault rifles Sturmgewehr 44

10   Degrelle, op. cit., p. 330.

54.   The 1st Platoon leader from the 2nd Company, *Kampfgruppe 'Derriks'* during the fighting for Dąbie [Altdamm]. (Charles Verpoorten's collection)

- 4 heavy machine guns Maschinengewehr 42
- 60 machine pistols Maschinenpistole 40
- 16 mortars Granatenwerfer 34, calibre 88 mm, which were left behind by the troops decommissioned earlier

Organisation of the *SS-Kampfgruppe 'Derriks'*:
Three assault companies:

- 1st Company: *SS-Untersturmführer* Andre Regibeau
  - ◊ 1st Platoon: *SS-Untersturmführer* Daniel Wouters
  - ◊ 2nd Platoon: *SS-Hauptscharfuhrer* Pierre Hancisse (WIA 17/03/1945)
  - ◊ 3rd Platoon: *SS-Hauptscharfuhrer* Maxime Havet (WIA), Chavanne (WIA), *SS-Untersturmführer* Jacques Leroy
- 2nd Company: *SS-Untersturmführer* Mathieu de Coster
  - ◊ 1st Platoon: *SS-Untersturmführer* Jean Piron
  - ◊ 2nd Platoon: *SS-Untersturmführer* Maurice Deravet
  - ◊ 3rd Platoon: *SS-Untersturmführer* Abel Delannoy
- 3rd Company: *SS-Obersturmführer* Leon Gillis
  - ◊ 1st Platoon: *SS-Untersturmführer* Eduard Serlet
  - ◊ 2nd Platoon: *SS-Untersturmführer* Jean Hallebardier

55. A member of the Knight's Cross of the Iron Cross Order, SS-Obersturmführer Leon Gillis. (Michel le Roy's collection)

- ◊ 3rd Platoon: *SS-Untersturmführer* GePe (WIA)
- • 4th Company (heavy): *SS-Obersturmführer* Henri Thyssen
  - ◊ 1st Platoon: *SS-Untersturmführer* Roger Gondry (two MG42 teams + mortars)
  - ◊ 2nd Platoon: *SS-Untersturmführer* Georges Suain (four MG42 teams)
  - ◊ 3rd Platoon: *SS-Untersturmführer* Louis Bervaes (four mortar teams)
  - ◊ 4th Platoon: *SS-Untersturmführer* Rene Serlet (KIA 18/03/1945).[11]

As we can see, the formation had an experienced and battle-tested cadre. All these men were volunteers, ready to throw themselves into fire alongside their commanders – and many of them became famous as exemplary warriors. Leon Degrelle upheld their passionate belief that the enemy's advance could still be stopped. The day before deployment, he awarded medals for their fight in Pomerania – and the action did not make them wait long. The Russians renewed their offensive quickly and the Dąbie bridgehead was their main target.

---

11 de Bruyne, Rikmenspoel, op. cit., p. 291.

Meanwhile, the Walloon reserve units, commanded by *SS-Hauptsturmführer* Jules Mathieu, had been moved to the western bank of the Oder, to a town called Bergholz, where they remained until the end of April 1945. Leon Degrelle and his staff set their command post in Brussow castle belonging to the von Mackensen family, 30 kilometres west of Szczecin. From that moment on, not including a few isolated propagandist visitations, he remained behind the main battle line, as he was concentrating on the events foreshadowing the end of the war.[12]

Battle for the bridgehead – outline of the area of combat

Before we begin to describe the last battles the Walloon volunteers fought, we should first characterise the natural environment they had found themselves in. The region of this battle was vividly described by Roland Devresse:

> Between Gryfice [Greifenhagen] and Szczecin [Stettin], the Oder waters flow wide, three to five kilometres, isolating the flat plains rolling in the west and cracked in the east. The river forks into many wide and winding branches. It flows over sandbars and swampy little islands, groves thickly overgrown and unwelcoming.
>
> By Szczecin, the Oder's arms divide in a wide river-mouth and disappear into waterlogged polder terrain. The river's current is rather strong in the spring. Similar to the Baltic Sea, Oder is indifferent to the flows.
>
> Szczecin is a city that has 270 000 inhabitants,[13] a very important sea-port. Docks, tanks and scrapyards are strategically located between the two river-arms. It's an old Hanseatic[14] city, lording on the left bank, greatly scarred by numerous Anglo-American air-raids. It is surrounded by modern suburbs. There is a sense of comfort to the picturesque suburban area. It's a fortified steady stronghold, enclosed by double ramparts, ten to fifteen metres wide. There are army and naval garrisons, about thirty thousand men strong.[15]

---

12 Ibid.
13 The current number of Szczecin inhabitants is 385,000 – data for 06/10/2013.
14 Hansa – a coalition of Northern European trade cities in the Middle Ages and the early modern period.
15 Devresse, Roland, *Les Volontaires se la Jeunesse a la Legion Wallonie*, vol. 14, p. 73.

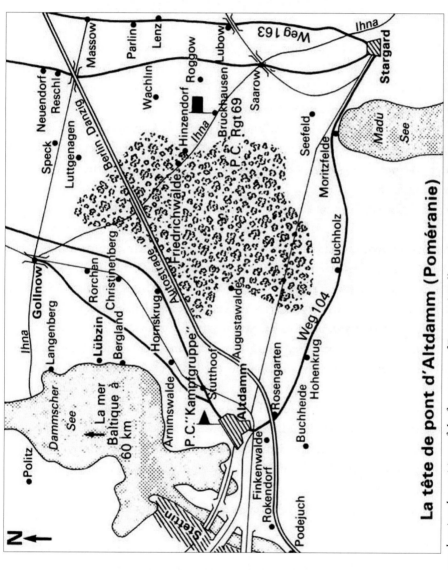

La tête de pont d'Altdamm (Poméranie)

56. A map showing the positions of the formations of Division *'Wallonien'* around Dąbie [Altdamm]. (Charles Verpoorten's collection)

7

Harbingers of the Fall

It had been brewing for the past couple of days and it finally came on 14 March 1945. Marshal Zhukov's armies had launched a violent assault on the Dąbie bridgehead, defended by the tail-end of the III *SS Panzer* Corps (Germanic), led by Lieutenant General Martin Unrein.[1]

The next day, the *'Wallonien'* and *'Langemarck' Kampfgruppe*s were put on high alert and deployed to Szczecin to man the newly-formed defence line. A day later, *SS-Sturmbannführer* Henri Derriks and his men reached the rally point in Szczecin docks.

The general situation could be described as tragic. During the first phase of the battle, the 24th *SS-Panzergrenadier* Regiment *'Danmark'* from *'Nordland'* Division had shrunk to some 50 men. Their commanding officer, *SS-Obersturmbannführer* Krugel, was killed in the battle for the Dąbie railway station. The Danes were relieved by two Flemish companies. The 10th *SS Panzer* Regiment from *'Frundsberg'* Division was equipped with just a few tanks. Its CO, *SS-Obersturmbannführer* Otto Paetsch, was fatally wounded.

On the evening of 16 March, the Walloons were ordered to back the 281st *Wehrmacht* Infantry Division entrenched between Dąbie and Klęskowo [Hockendorf].[2] The Walloons were tasked with securing a breach, 1,200 metres long. *SS-Sturmbannführer* Henri Derriks deployed his 1st Company to Kijewo [Rosengarten],[3] while the 2nd Company was to rendezvous with the German forces on the left flank. The 3rd Company was kept in the reserves behind a railway embankment nearby and the 4th Company took positions even further left.[4]

According to Jean Mabire, the evening went as follows:

16 March 1045, 8 PM. Flames illuminated the entire scenery. Dancing fires lighted red flashes on the silhouettes of soldiers approaching the lines, heavily

---

1   It is an interesting fact that the CO of the *SS Panzer* Corps was a general from the *Wehrmacht*, not the *Waffen-SS*.
2   Klęskowo – currently a district of Szczecin.
3   Currently a housing estate (*osiedle*) within Szczecin's administrative boundaries.
4   de Bruyne, Eddy, Rikmenspoel, Mark, *For Rex and Belgium ...* (Solihull, 2004), p. 291.

57.   Szczecin [Stettin] Docks, 16 March 1945 – a few hours before battle. Second
on the left is *SS-Untersturmführer* Jacques Leroy (3rd Platoon Leader in the 1st
Company) – grievously wounded during the battle for Cherkassy; he lost an eye
and his right arm. The photograph shows him wearing a private's clasp (probably
because it was easier to unclasp using one hand, than an officer's clasp). He is
accompanied by the Commanding Officer of the 1st Company, *Kampfgruppe 'Derriks'*,
SS-Untersturmführer Andre Regibeau. The two young boys are the messengers
of the Company Commander. First on the left is a Frenchman, Robert Thuillez,
and second on the right is Marcel Leplae. (Eddy de Bruyne's collection)

burdened with weapons and ammunition. As *Kampfgruppe 'Derriks'* closed
in on Altdamm, the artillery fire escalated. The newly-arrived quickly moved
among the ranks. Divided into small teams set wide apart, they entered the
danger-zone. The night had already fallen and the exploding shells illuminated
the terrain to the point where it was light as day and it was easy to maintain
communications. Never before had the Burgundians faced such overwhelming
artillery fire. The whole sky was ablaze. Explosions came one by one and never
eased up for the entire duration of the battle for the bridgehead.[5]

The rest of the night passed in relative calm, in an unending and steady thunder

---

5   Mabire, Jean, *Division de Choc Wallonie, Lutte á Mort en Poméranie* (ed. Jacques Grancher, 1996), p.
211.

of bombs. Far ahead of the railway embankment, grenadiers from the 1st and 2nd Company had dug several holes to form reinforced battle stations before the dawn came. Neither Regibeau nor de Coster knew where they were exactly on that wide and unfriendly plain, naked and smooth like a pool table.[6]

At around 1:00 a.m. on the night of 17 March, the 1st Company was moved and relocated to the fields running down Kijewo's woods, towards the sugar factory in Dąbie. The positions vacated by the 1st Company had been taken by a company of the *Wehrmacht*, whose complement was reduced to some 20 men by the morning. The 3rd and 4th Company formed a second defence line and an anti-tank barricade by the sandy hills and the railway embankment, between Dąbie railway station and Szczecin Zdroje [Finkenwalde].[7]

When dawn came on 17 March, the 1st Company's situation was degrading quickly, even critical. The soldiers, having found no protection in the terrain whatsoever, were unable to build even the smallest semblance of a trench, not to mention any serious entrenchments. They were the perfect target for a frontal assault that the Soviets had launched from the woods nearby. *SS-Untersturmführer* Andre Regibeau and his men had to practically bite the ground under violent fire. Their fierce resistance, however, costed them numerous casualties.[8]

Once again we shall cite Jean Mabire's epic narration, which allows us to recreate the nature of that battle:

> At dawn officer cadet Jacques Leroy arrived at Lieutenant Regibeau's command post to report on the location of his platoon, opposite the Rosengarten woods. 'Alright, Jacques', said the 1st Company's CO. 'Now get back to your platoon. The Russians might attack any moment.'
>
> Just as Leroy left his cover, he saw tanks on his right out of the corner of his eye. They were advancing in four rows, perpendicularly to the company's command post. He started to count. There were ... nineteen of them! And they were Soviet, no doubt. What could a miserable cripple[9] do, alone on that road, barely several dozen metres from those steel monstrosities? Luckily for him,

---

6   Ibid., p. 214.
7   de Bruyne, Rikmenspoel, op. cit., p. 292.
8   Ibid.
9   During a fierce battle to break out of the Cherkassy Cauldron, Leroy was grievously wounded – losing his right eye and right arm, which had to be amputated. By a stroke of luck his comrades managed to evacuate him to the field hospital. After a long convalescence at the beginning of 1945 Leroy returned to his unit.

58.   *SS-Untersturmführer* Jacques Leroy – Eastern Front, beginning of 1944. (Michel le Roy's collection)

the tanks had no infantry support. Leroy saw in the twilight the gun turret of the closest tank slowly turn towards him. He didn't even have time to fall to the ground when the shot came. Blinding flash. Sound of explosion. The shell luckily flew above his head. Leroy jumped to the railway embankment to take cover.

The enemy tank's crew wasn't keen on wasting their ammo on a single man. The platoon commander ran towards his men. An empty sleeve slipped from his belt and fluttered behind him.

'Russian tanks!' Leroy yelled, when he got to his men. 'Dig in, deep as you can!'

'How can we stop them, lieutenant?'

'I was promised *panzerfausts*. They'll send some from the rear.'

True enough, a horse-cart delivered the weapons which, for some inexplicable reason, were just barrels missing fuses which were supposed to be delivered from somewhere else but apparently forgotten.

Were the Burgundians to attack tanks empty-handed?

Captain Derriks was just about to move the 1st and 2nd Companies' main posts which had been too fore-reached when the battle broke out with

59.   An early headshot of Jacques
Leroy. (J.L. Roba's collection)

incredible fury. Groups of Russians were swarming out of the woods. They attacked screaming savagely.

The Walloons gave as good as they got. For now they had enough ammo to maintain hellish fire. The enemy was forced back, but they were supported by some twenty T-34 tanks, which were closing in on the defence positions of *Kampfgruppe 'Derriks'*. Russian armoured cars appeared on the wide plain, west from the road from Altdamm and they were passing by the company's forward positions, commanded by Andre Regibeau. Hidden in their foxholes, the Burgundians were unable to use their *panzerfausts* and they had to let them go through.

Officer cadet Thierry Hancisse, 2nd Platoon's leader, rushed to the command post of the 1st Company to inform Lieutenant Regibeau that the enemy had infiltrated his platoon's sector. At that moment a shell exploded right next to him. The young NCO collapsed, clutching his leg. His commander dragged him to the back, to a building some hundred metres away. There were more wounded Burgundians there. Hancisse was in great pain. 'You want a smoke?' his CO asked. Hancisse smoked cigarette after cigarette, huge drops of sweat falling down his pale face where scars from old wounds formed livid

blue lines. The veteran had participated in almost every battle of the Walloon Legion. Past battles had wrought deep marks on his body. Now his shin was badly broken. The medics quickly put him in a small wheelchair and evacuated him under the cover of some trees.[10]

SS-Untersturmführer Jacques Leroy's platoon not only withstood heavy assault from Soviet infantry but also managed to destroy several T-34s and stop the enemy in their sector, while still maintaining their positions for 72 hours. For that feat, *SS-Untersturmführer* Leroy was later nominated for the Knight's Cross Iron Cross (*Ritterkreuz des Eisernen Kreuzes*).[11]

Leon Degrelle, in that particular tone of his, describes the tragedy of the fighting and the Leroy brothers' heroism:

The casualties were terrible: in three days our sector lost sixty percent of its defenders, who had been either killed or wounded. Dug in in their foxholes, only their heads or arms sticking out, they got hit by the shrapnel from shells or grenades mostly in the face. They would run then to my tiny command post with terrifying bloody holes where their jaws used to be. Often their tongues would still stick out, pink and trembling, unnaturally long.

Twenty-five or thirty wounded would run to me at a time. Some of them, who were hit while on the run, had metal shrapnel in their groins, they would convulse horribly, screaming in agony. But I had to command, had to keep an eye on everything, despite the stench of curdling blood and excrements that floated over wet trenches.[12]

We had this young officer in the 'Derriks', very thin and pale, Lieutenant Leroy from Binche, who had enlisted when he was sixteen. A year earlier, during the fighting in Cherkassy, he lost his right arm and eye. But he wanted to go back to the anti-Soviet front so badly. He was a communications officer. The invalid's presence among the soldiers was touching.

Leroy's brother was a platoon leader. He got killed on the embankment in Finkenwalde three days before the end of the Oder battle. Our young cripple didn't break under the pain of his loss, but immediately asked to take his brother's place. I agreed. It as an incredible and amazing sight: a cripple with a mangled torso fiercely fighting hand-to-hand for three days and three nights,

---

10   Mabire, op. cit., pp. 216-217.
11   de Bruyne, Rikmenspoel, op. cit., p. 292.
12   Degrelle, Leon, *Front Wschodni 1941-1945* (Międzyzdroje, 2002), p. 332.

60.   Eduard Serlet – 1st Platoon Leader in the 3rd Company, *Kampfgruppe 'Derriks'* during the battle for the Dąbie Bridgehead [Altdamm]. Here he is photographed as a soldier in the Walloon Legion. (Michel le Roy's collection)

firing his machine pistol, which he operated quite handily with his left arm.[13]

In the afternoon, Andre Regibeau's company managed to break out of the Red Army's iron pincers. During the morning's fighting, however, they had lost a fourth of their complement (about 30 men) and were temporarily moved to the reserves. The 2nd Company replaced them and, just like their comrades before them, suffered a hailstorm of Soviet shells. Despite that, they still managed to eliminate several of the enemy tanks in heavy battle. Jean Mabire, already quoted several times here, describes one of the skirmishes of the 2nd Company's 3rd Platoon, led by *SS-Untersturmführer* Abel Delannoy:

In the late morning, the Russians futilely tried to break into the Burgundian sector. Abel Delannoy's men were ordered to move to new battle stations, at the opposite end of the Walloon sector. Between ruined buildings they met an old woman in black, who decided to stay on that patch of ground that had always been her home. With empty eyes she watched the soldiers as they passed her by.

---

13   Ibid., p. 334.

Did she even realise they weren't Germans but Belgian volunteers?

The Burgundians took their positions behind the railway embankment, which was the focal point of their defence. German guns were shooting the last of their ammo and returning quickly. The area was becoming very dangerous.

'Intervals! Intervals!' the NCOs kept shouting, wanting to spread their men as much as possible before steel and fire started raining on their positions. A dull thunder of the first salvo shook the scenery. The shock-wave pinned the grenadiers in their trenches. [The] acrid stench of explosions was everywhere. The ground shook relentlessly under the fire like a sick man in fever. An entire Walloon team, positioned too tightly, was mowed down by one shell. Mangled corpses strewn the ground. Merokx, Abel Delannoy's batman, a volunteer who accompanied his commanding officer, was hit by shrapnel. He became deathly pale. Blood gushed from his arm. Another communications officer was killed by a shell on a yard of a house at the rear. From the first morning of the battle for the Altdamm bridgehead the casualties had been terrible.[14]

On 18 March, the heavy shelling of the Soviet artillery renewed. The 2nd Company, exhausted in earlier skirmishes, fell back to rest a bit in a calmer and safer place behind the railway embankment. Time after time the Russians covered German positions with incredibly dense fire. The soldiers of the 10th *SS Panzer* Division *'Frundsberg'*, in spite of their disastrous position, fought with their Walloon comrades arm-in-arm with great devotion, defending their posts on the hills west of Szczecin Zdroje. Meanwhile, two mortar platoons from the 4th (heavy) Company from *Kampfgruppe 'Derriks'* were able to launch a small counter-attack, halting the enemy for the time being. The leader of the 4th Platoon, *SS-Untersturmführer* Rene Serlet, paid for it with his life. Because of the continuous pressure from the enemy, *SS-Sturmbannführer* Henri Derriks was forced to move his command post west, to a basement of one of the houses in Dąbie. By the evening of 18 March, the Walloons were able to hold their positions but their forces were dwindling fast.[15]

One of the main characters in the 28th *SS*-Volunteer Grenadier Division *'Wallonien'* was Father Gerard Stockman, a Catholic priest serving as the formation's chaplain. Since most of the soldiers were fervent Catholics, *SS-Reichsführer* Heinrich Himmler allowed the priest to accompany the division.[16]

---

14 Mabire, op. cit., p. 222.
15 de Bruyne, Rikmenspoel, op. cit., p. 293.
16 The author knows of only one more example of a priest serving in an *SS* division. That division was the

61.   A less-known photograph of
SS-Sturmbannführer Henri Derriks.
(Eddy de Bruyne's collection)

In one of Jean Mabire's stories, based on memories of one of the veterans, we can read of Father Gerard's charisma:

> The platoon leader ran for twenty metres and jumped into a relatively deep trench. Now the railway embankment, the only cover on this flat plain, was now behind him. Before the embankment were the Russian tanks. The bombardment continued with small breaks. Now and again they could hear rounds of machine guns. GePe was now halfway to the PAK.[17] He had to get to it but he wasn't crazy about being out in the open. Suddenly, he spotted a man walking towards him. His steady step, wide back a little bent, his arms crossed on his chest. *'Wallonien'* Division's chaplain, Father Gerard Stockman, indifferent to enemy fire, came to visit his lambs. The old Trappist[18] seemed to completely ignore the danger he was in. He approached GePe easily and handed him a couple of cigarettes.
>
> 'Where are your men?' he asked the officer.

33rd *SS*-Grenadier Division *'Charlemagne'* and Monseigneur Jean de Mayol de Lupe.

17   *Panzerabwehrkanone* – an anti-tank gun. There were only a few versions of the model.

18   Trappists, the Order of Cistersians of the Strict Observance – a Catholic order known by that name since 1903, originating from the Cistersian Abby La Trappe in the northern part of the Centre Region of France.

62. Two pages from Father Gerard Stockman's '*Soldbuch*'. It is an interesting fact that he had served as a high-ranking *SS-Sturmbannführer*. (Eddy de Bruyne's collection)

'Behind the embankment, father.'

'I will go see them, then.'

The chaplain left the trench and headed for the train-tracks. He wasn't running or dodging bullets. He just calmly walked down the embankment, his silhouette standing out starkly. Once on the opposite side, he joined the grenadiers and artillery-men who were surprised and happy to see him emerge from the storm of steel and fire.'[19]

On 19 March, the Russians had focused their efforts on the right wing from Szczecin to Szczecin Zdroje and Szczecin to Podejuchy[20] [Podejuch], where they planned on launching the main assault. The villages were crushed under terrible bombardments and with no anti-aircraft protection, they could not be held. Hastily-gathered groups of marauders were being stopped by German military police *Feldpolizei* and sent back to the front-line. Everybody who didn't have sufficient argument for leaving their units, risked court martial – *Standgericht* –

---

19 Mabire, op. cit., p. 218.
20 Currently a district of Szczecin.

and a sentence: immediate execution by hanging on the closest tree.

Exhausted by the fight, the Walloons were allowed to retreat to the Dąbie bridgehead on 18 March at around 10:00 p.m. The bridge was being defended by a platoon of machine pistols from the 24th *SS-Panzergrenadier* Regiment *'Danmark'* of the 11th *SS-Panzergrenadier* Division *'Nordland'*. When the Danes had retreated, the bridge fell.[21] Fifteen-hundred metres south, the rearguard of *Kampfgruppe 'Derriks'* crossed the Oder with two German tanks on a railway bridge north of Szczecin Zdroje, blowing it up behind them.[22]

The last hours of the battle for the Dąbie bridgehead are described by Abel Delannoy:

> The field mail from Berlin delivered the Walloon daily 'Denevir', printed in Brussels, and chocolate: a rare treat in this sixth year of war! Our morale increased greatly and remains as high as it's ever been. I enlarged and perfected my foxhole. Hand grenades and ammunition I keep within reach. From time to time I empty a magazine at the ever bothersome Ivan. Night fell again, and with it the great shells meant to annihilate us, slowly but steadily. Three German tanks perched behind the embankment, their strafing weapons ready to give covering fire. I learned that the general retreat was already under-way. We would leave last, sitting on our tanks. To keep Zhukov's thugs unawares, we planned on launching a decoy attack with all the arms we had left. Hanging on the turrets, we can still make our guns spit long waves of deadly bullets. We flow towards heaven a little less riddled with steel. After three days and three nights only a third of my men remain relatively intact. We had crossed the Oder under a large bridge, just before we blew it up. In the darkness I couldn't see the corpses of German deserters, hanging on the bridge girders, wooden signs around their necks branding them *Feigling*![23]

In 72 hours of bloody skirmishes *Kampfgruppe 'Derriks'* had lost 110 men. Among the numerous wounded were officers such as *SS-Untersturmführer* Hallebardier, Lienart and GePe.[24] For his leadership during those difficult days, *SS-Sturmbannführer* Henri Derriks was awarded the German Cross in Gold.[25]

---

21   Landwehr, Richard, *The Wallonien – The History of...* (Bennington, 2006), p. 39.
22   Tieke, Wilhelm, *Tragedy of the Faithful. A History of the III. (Germanisches) SS-Panzer Korps* (J. J. Fedorowicz, 2001), p. 264.
23   Delannoy, Abel, *Confession d'un SS*, p. 49.
24   de Bruyne, Rikmenspoel, op. cit., p. 294.
25   Landwehr, op. cit., p. 40.

63. *SS-Untersturmführer* Robert de Goy – Henri Derriks's Adjutant. (Eddy de Bruyne's collection)

That was the end of the fight for the right bank of the Oder. It was also an end of the III *SS Panzer* Corps (Germanic) – a part of which was the *'Wallonien'* Division. Its combat strength was largely decreased and never rebuilt.[26] They had only broken regiments and battalions left. Some of the companies had the complement of a platoon. The Western Pomerania was lost.[27] German troops who were still fighting around Gdańsk [Danzig], the Hel Peninsula [Hela] and Królewiec [Konigsberg] couldn't influence the final outcome of the war any more. The besieged Courland was the same. In the west, the Allies were already deep into Germany. Mainz, Siegen, Frankfurt and Wurzburg had been taken. All that Hitler's armies had left was a feeble and vague hope to turn the tide of the war, either by political manoeuvring or by magic.[28]

---

26 Having suffered so many casualties, the III *SS Panzer* Corps moved to the reserves of the Army Group 'Vistula' and the 11th Army underwent reform. (ed.)

27 Simultaneously, Heinrich Himmler lost his command of the Army Group 'Vistula'. He passed it to Colonel General Heinrich on 21 March 1945. (ed.)

28 Tieke, op. cit., p. 264.

8

Oder. Life or Death!

On 22 March 1945, the Walloon battalion was deployed to Gut Schmagerow, 20 kilometres west of the Oder, to regroup and recuperate. *SS-Sturmbannführer* Hellebaut chose Gut Salzow as his command post, a town two kilometres south-west towards Locknitz. Leon Degrelle and his staff took quarters in the von Mackensen family's castle in Brussow and was desperately trying to figure out how to get his men out of the trap they found themselves in.[1]

On 1 April, the *'Wallonien'* Division's chaplain, Father Gerard – who held the rank of *SS-Sturmbannführer* – held Easter Mass. A great many soldiers attended. Game hunted in surrounding forests, as well as a mountain of flour luckily discovered in the Szczecin docks, allowed them to spend the day in joyous celebration.[2]

With his trademark humour and eloquence, Abel Delannoy thus describes this episode:

> We held a military parade and handed out medals. Our chaplain, Father Gerard, was awarded the Iron Cross for his quiet bravery which he had proven carrying the wounded out of the battlefield. He also held mass on the castle courtyard. Leon Degrelle gave a fiery speech. Between orations he announced: 'Today we'll get two thousands litres of wine, just for you, boys!' He was met with a long ovation from the ever-thirsty heroes. Like all true Burgundians, they were always ready to empty a force of chalices!
>
> On our way back to our quarters I intoned the hymn of our Legion: 'We are Legionnaires from our beloved country. The Motherland will be proud of our blood shed. Hum! Hum! Let us go without delay!'[3]

The next day, a couple hundred of Walloon workers from the Reichsarbeitsdienst came. Not one of them wanted to join the troops, so they

---

1   de Bruyne, Eddy, Rikmenspoel, Mark, *For Rex and Belgium ...* (Solihull, 2004), p. 295.
2   Devresse, Roland, *Les Volontaires de la Jeunesse ...* , vol. 15, p. 6.
3   Delannoy, Abel, *Confession d'un SS*, p. 49.

64.   *SS-Hauptsturmführer* Jean Vermeire.
Sepp Dietrich is shown on the left – one
of the legendary *Waffen-SS* commanders.
(Eddy de Bruyne's collection)

were directed to building anti-tank ditches and other reinforcements along with the soldiers who refused to continue the fighting. They were supervised by *SS-Hauptsturmführer* Jean Vermeire. Richard Landwehr, author of *The Wallonien*, has a different take on the subject and argues that the workers enlisted in the formation enthusiastically and began combat training.[4] This hypothesis should not be taken too seriously, however.

In his memoirs, still awaiting print, Freddy Jacques speaks of the new recruits' arrival:

> For several days we had been waiting for an assignment and finally we moved to Plowen, where a new battalion was being formed. I found out these men were 'recruits', youths deported from German factories. Degrelle – sheer insanity – incorporated them into the Legion under the pretence that at least they will have enough to eat and will avoid the bad atmosphere of the work camps [sic]. For me, personally, it was a huge moral dilemma. When you think about it, I still accepted the platoon's command, though. First day, I gathered the men and told them: 'Gentlemen, I am aware of the manner of your arrival here. I

---

4   Landwehr, Richard, *The Wallonien – The History of…* (Bennington, 2006), p. 41.

65.   Freddy Jacques – photographed here as an SS-*Unterscharführer*. (Michel le Roy's collection)

know you have been drafted against your will and I understand your situation well. What I don't know is what they want to do with you. I dare not speculate that you will be sent to the front. The programme for the next weeks is this: we continue to train. And train we will, as long as possible, to buy time. You know the general situation as well as I do and you understand that the end of the war is near. I ask you to be patient for a couple of weeks more. A lot will happen here! And I won't stand in your way, to the contrary. But I do ask for a little of good will on your part and everything will go well. If not, come to me.'[5]

Here are Roland Devresse's comments:

The speech worked because the front was far away. The exercises were more like training for keeping up shape. Captain Vermeire was building a reservist battalion which was never to fight on the front. Personally, I played my role just like my friend Freddy Jacques. Unable to bare this ridiculous situation, I asked for assignment with the *'Derriks'*. Two days later I was on my way to Schmagerow. I was supposed to join that one combat-able formation.[6]

---

5   Jacques, Freddy, *Mémoires*.
6   Devresse, op. cit., p. 4.

Story 1: Illustrations tell the story of the preparations for battle and the sacrifice of Jacques Capelle's company, which occurred during Operation '*Sonnenwende*' on the Lindenberg hill.

The 7th Company anxiously prepare themselves for the forthcoming assault to be launched from Kolin.

The assault will be supported by the MG42 team of the 69th Regiment of the 'Wallonien' Division, as well as by a German armoured train.

Thanks to the element of surprise, the Walloons managed to take over Lindenberg.

Their next mission was to hold Lindenberg for 24 hours.

The night was calm. The sun rose and suddenly, an intense shelling erupted.

Soviet soldiers – supported by tanks – launched a deadly assault to recover Lindenberg. *SS-Untersturmführer* Jacques Poels was killed while attacking a Soviet T-34 with a *panzerfaust*.

La 7eme compagnie est encerclée Hauptsturmführer

The Walloons managed to hold Lindenberg for 27 hours before the 7th Company was completely annihilated.

SS-Obersturmführer Capelle died shortly after the first Soviet troops had reached his position. He managed to send a final message to *SS-Sturmbannführer* Frans Hellebaut: *"C'est fini, monsieur le commandeur, ils sont là."* ("It's over, Mr Commander, they are here.")

Story 2: The drawings show the events in Rosówek [Neu-Rosow], where many Burgundians were injured or killed on 23 April 1945. The fate of some of them (Albert Verpoorten's included) remains unknown even today.

23 April 1945: Kampfgruppe 'Derriks' asks for 20 volunteers to protect the Walloon and Flemish retreat around Rosówek [Neu-Rosow].

SS-Unterstturmführer Albert Verpoorten joins his fellow comrades – including Jean Hallebardier and Roger Gondry – in a defensive position before the Soviets launch their attack.

The Soviets have no intention of remaining inactive – deciding to use their heavy artillery to shell fragile positions. Verpoorten tries to find a safe place within an improvised trench.

In the trench, Verpoorten finds his friend, SS-Oberstturmführer GePe, and two other soldiers. Suddenly, the position is brought down by a terrible explosion.

Mon bras …. mon bras ….

The author chose to keep the original writings in the comics, as prepared by Stephane 'Godus' Gosselin, in English and French. Godus's works can be viewed and purchased on his website: <http://www.unejeunessefrancaise.blogspot.com/>

The two soldiers die instantly. Verpoorten is alive, but seriously wounded. Only GePe manages to leave the position (helped by a Flemish volunteer) and returns to the headquarters of *Kampfgruppe 'Derriks'* – marching 1.5 km in the cold.

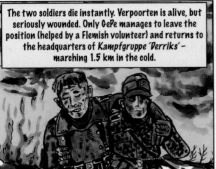

Godverdomm' !!! Il faut envoyer tout de suite un infirmier sur place!

GePe tells Derriks what has happened to the small group of soldiers in the trench before collapsing. Derriks immediately decides to send one medic to the position, but unfortunately, the medic is killed before he reaches them.
Finally, Derriks decides to go himself to the positon to see if he can find any survivors.

Unfortunately, it's too late. As Derriks and his men reach the position, they find their comrades dead – identifying them through their papers. Among them were *SS-Untersturmführer* Albert Verpoorten and *SS-Scharführer* Bayard

PART 1

1a, 1b, 1c: The aimer of an MG42 – an *SS-Sturmmann* from *Kampfgruppe 'Derriks'*; first half of April 1945, Gut Schmagerow. The soldier is wearing a wool uniform M43 and is equipped with the typical gear of infantry sub-units: a foldable entrenching tool, a breadbag and a canteen. Equipment also includes a camouflage tent sheet *Eichenlaubmuster* (type A). Instead of a helmet, he wears a camouflage cap sewn from the *Platanenmuster* material (type ½). The sleeve of his uniform tunic shows his rank insignia. The soldier does not have any insignia indicating his national formation being a part of the *Waffen-SS*. (Łukasz Dyczkowski)

2a, 2b, 2c: The munitions officer of an MG42 – an *SS-Sturmmann* from *Kampfgruppe 'Derriks'*; first half of April 1945, Gut Schmagerow. The soldier is wearing a broadcloth uniform M43 and a set sewn from drill material covered with polka-dot camouflage, *Erbsentarnmuster*. It is worthy of note that he wears the camouflage jacket underneath the wool jacket. In the majority of available photographs, the *Waffen-SS* soldiers wear them over the wool uniform. The basic equipment hangs on webbing suspenders and a leather main belt. The entrenching tool is placed in a cover made from *Presstoff* (commonly known in Poland as *'preszpan'*), which shows it was made late into the war. The soldier is armed with an MG42, known as the *Trommel*. (Łukasz Dyczkowski)

PART 2

The following photographs were taken especially for this edition. The photoshoot took place during the re-enactment in Rosówek (Neu-Rosow) near where the Walloons fought in battle in April 1945. The photographed individuals wear uniforms and equipment that were in use in these particular battles. The models are from the 'Pomerania 1945' re-enacting group.

1. Two soldiers in front of a captured Soviet T-34 tank. The first is Walloon; the second one (on the right) is Flemish from the 27th *SS*-Volunteer Division *'Langemarck'*. The Walloons and the Flemish fought alongside one another during the fighting near Rosówek. The Flemish volunteer – aside from the standard-issue grenadier's gear – is also equipped with a *Panzerfaust*. The standout element of his uniform jacket is a national armshield showing the Flanders emblem: the Flemish Lion. (Tomasz Borowski)

2. An *SS-Sturmmann* from an MG42 heavy machine gun crew. His M43-type uniform jacket shows a national armshield worn by Walloon volunteers. This pattern was common in the *Waffen-SS*. His M42 helmet is smeared with mud so as not to reflect light, as well as making the soldier less visible to the enemy. (Tomasz Borowski)

3. This Walloon *SS-Untersturmführer* wears a national armshield of the first type on his sleeve. Aside from combat awards used by the German *Wehrmacht*, he also wears the Walloon Blood Order. (Tomasz Borowski)

4. The Walloon on the left is armed with a Czech-manufactured machine gun (ZB26). This was a unique weapon used by the German Army – also known as MG26(t). The Flemish *SS-Grenadier* on the right wears a camouflage protection sheet *Zeltbahn* made of camouflage cloth, pattern oak *Eichenlaubmuster* (type A). (Tomasz Borowski)

4bb. Walloon *SS-Unterscharführer*. He wears HBT polka dot camouflage, Erbsentarnmuster, old-style marching boots and breeches. On his head he has a single button enlisted man's cap. He is armed with the well-known MP-40 machine pistol. Magazines for his weapon are placed in a an olive/black pouch. (Tomasz Borowski)

'Profile' pictures by Łukasz Dyczkowski, see https://www.tropiciel-historii.pl/.

'Profile' pictures by Łukasz Dyczkowski, see https://www.tropiciel-historii.pl/.

These facts are confirmed by Leon Degrelle:

I chose to assign the remnants of my division to the second reservist regiment, which was comprised of the sick and injured and old Legionnaires, useless at the front-line.

For a short time the unit was also home to a group of a hundred of our countrymen, who had been working in the Reich's factories. Some dim-witted officer in a fit of madness decided to dress them in German uniforms and sent them to us, not even bothering to ask their permission.

We were a Volunteer Legion. I had no intention of sending them into battle or even keeping them in uniform. They were brave men, who may have disagreed with our views, but they were forced to come here. I ordered them to be supplied with rations for three days and some cigarettes. One of my officers led them to the rear. Every one of them received a demobilisation slip.

Some time later I evacuated the sick and lightly wounded. The rest were holding on with their last strength. Those, who would only hinder us in these last battles, we preferred to save and send away in time from that Soviet abyss. It might've been against regulations, but I paid no mind and signed a file of marching orders. Two-hundred men unable to fight started towards Rostock, an old Baltic port.

Discreetly, by all means necessary, I was ridding myself of the ballast, trying to soften the final blow.[7]

To close this matter, we quote Freddy Jacques once again:

We were soon sent to some town in order to take positions in the trenches dug by Russian women, whom the Organisation Todt treated like slaves.[8] We had to intervene several times, trying to make those thugs act a little more humane. In return we received thanks and smiles from the ladies. We were ordered to take positions on the third or fourth line, where there was no more danger. But the nearness of the front paralysed these people and they made it no secret that if the Russians came, I would have to keep them in line by force. Many times I asked the battalion's command to do something about it. It was unacceptable to send these poor recruits to the front-lines. As volunteers, we can take it. We

---

7   Degrelle, Leon, *Front Wschodni 1941-1945* (Międzyzdroje, 2002), p. 338.
8   Formed in 1938 in the Nazi Germany, this organisation's mandate was to build military installations. In the beginning it was supervised by Fritz Todt.

66.   Leon Degrelle awarding his officers the Iron Cross, First Class during a
ceremony celebrating their return from the Cherkassy Cauldron. First on the
left is *SS-Hauptsturmführer* Marcel Bonniver. (Michel le Roy's collection)

found ourselves in hell of our own volition, but them ... ! Captain Vermeire
promised to do everything he could.[9]

Sometime later, these recruits received demobilisation certificates, rations
for three days and cigarettes and were allowed to leave the ranks of the unit.
Some of them, probably too afraid to be on their own in a country plunged
into chaos, asked permission to stay. Some of them even fought in the coming
battles. After the war they were made to pay for it dearly, since even those recruits,
who had never volunteered, had great trouble avoiding trial and sentencing for
collaboration after their return to Belgium.[10]

The Burgundians who survived the last of the fighting and were willing to
continue on, spent their time leisurely warming up in the spring sun in their
comfortable quarters. They didn't want to think of their uncertain future too
much and so they lived day by day, as best as they could. *SS-Sturmbannführer*

9   Jacques, op. cit.
10   Devresse, op. cit., p. 4.

Hellebaut started reorganising. There was only one unit left that had some kind of coherence: Derriks's battalion, resting in a village estate. On around 7 April, Hellebaut proceeded to rebuild his formation, trying to create a *Kampfgruppe* in the strength of two battalions.[11]

> Captain Bonniver used the occasion to rebuild the second battalion in Bismarck. At his disposal he had a grenadier regiment, comprised of his own choice officers, as well as the support of Mirgain's pioneer company, who had just arrived, well equipped in Czechoslovakia. Soon I was able to form the last combat-worthy *Kampfgruppe*, under my own command.[12]

Let us go back to Schmagerow. Many Burgundians, who had spent time in that place, retained singular memories of it. Here are a couple of words from *SS-Untersturmführer* GePe who, wounded in Dąbie, returned to his unit after his convalescence.

> After setting up a meeting to discuss my treatment, the doctor stopped me in Schmagerow, in front of the castle, and said, 'Go inside, you'll find everyone there'. (...) He was right, they were all there (...). I shook hands and got pats on the back. I greeted Captain Derriks appropriately, not expecting much from him. I quickly understood why it would've been better if he just remained sitting: he kept taking out his revolver and pointing it at me. Half an hour later I found a harmonium – every self-respecting castle had to have one – and started playing. I saw Regibeau, de Coster, Monfils and many others. And I saw this girl, too, Karine, they called her. Later I learned she was a French writer, working as a journalist. Many of us tried to get her attention ...

Roland Devresse continues on the subject:

> This description bring us into the atmosphere of the officers' corps at the time. Derriks the Policeman calling the tune! A certain Karine will be considered as Mata Hari because she was suspected of being an agent of the Gestapo. Reality blurs with illusion. In this dark atmosphere of gods everything was possible!
> Life is good in Gut Schmagerow. Officers are resting, their men as well: no training, only one assembly a day, excellent supply of food. The Russians had

---

11 Ibid., p. 3.
12 Hellebaut, *La Drame de l'Europe de l'est*.

forgotten all about them, not a single plane in the sky, while the front-line is but 30 kilometres away, on the other side of Oder.

And that was when I arrived. I was welcomed nicely. I didn't know too many people and I didn't have too many contacts among the officers present, with the exception of Andre Regibeau who had helped me after I joined the *Kampfgruppe*. He still remembered me from Neweklau. I suggested de Coster should make me a platoon leader in the 2nd Company, a position vacated after Abel Delannoy had left. His and Derriks's and de Coster's goodbyes were rather cold.

From the very first moments after my return to the Legion, I was met with one surprise after another. First, there were these 'recruits', the strangest volunteers. And now I found myself in a camp, 'Pancho Villa'-style.[13] There was this South American atmosphere in Gut Schmagerow, where nothing was normal, especially when it comes to our military formation in the style of the *SS*. Officers were riding horses, and they were no gauchos. Derriks taking daily trips with a Pomeranian coach. The castle stables were well equipped.

The first thing every unit thinks of is to eat well. This was the case here, too. The general mood was nothing like the typical garrison life. Some assemblies were called just to keep up appearances, somebody was cleaning their gun from time to time. Aside from that – beautiful life. I quickly realised there was nothing I could do but join in. I got to know the men in my platoon a little. A week after my arrival in this paradise, we had to leave towards Oder. The Russians were mounting yet another offensive ... [14]

The reasons for Abel Delannoy's removal from the centre of the 'proper' *Kampfgruppe*, under Henri Derriks's command, can be found in his own memories with a definite note of sarcasm:

I like Schmagerow. I'm here with my platoon. No distinctions or ranks, only my men and me, living under one banner, eating the same things. Individual Christmas packages arrive three months late, damaged beyond belief. Unpacked, they were very tempting to the army's support personnel who were distributing those pricey sweets, not without malfeasance, I'm sure. To make sure that

---

13 Pancho Villa – a leader of Mexican peasants' *guerrilla* – a general during the Mexican revolution. Devresse means that the camp's atmosphere was rather loose and particular, different from the usual habits of the *Waffen-SS*.

14 Devresse, op. cit., pp. 7-8.

didn't happen, I conspired with two other platoon leaders and we improvised a small coup d'etat. We invaded the warehouse and ordered the personnel to prepare all the bottles, bags of sweets and cigarettes for direct dispensation of goods. They definitely did not like such quick distribution. The quartermaster went off to cry into the commandant's sleeve. The commandant said he was right to be upset. After all, the solidarity of quartermasters and bookkeepers is supposed to be beyond discussion! My failed *putsch* was probably the reason for my reassignment to the 3rd Battalion, which was mostly comprised of the various 'recruits'.[15] Supposedly, because I was a good infantry instructor. I took my leave from my CO,[16] who said to me, 'Delannoy, with eyes like yours you always go back to the *Kampfgruppe!*' Myself, I think he really meant: 'Delannoy, with eyes like yours, without a shred of consideration, you cannot remain in my *Kampfgruppe*'. There was nothing glamorous about serving with the 'recruits'. No heart in sight anywhere. For example, we were in trenches on the third line. My mercenaries refused to take the night watch so I had to replace them with two or three of the volunteers. Our commander visited us on 20 April 1945, the *Fuhrer's* last birthday, and described the heroic assault of the Walloons and the Flemish around Pommelen – Schillersdorf. I was cursing dreadfully for missing the games yet again.[17]

In short, in the middle of April 1945 the survivors of the 28th *SS*-Volunteer Grenadier Division *'Wallonien'* were scattered around various towns behind the Oder River. The engineering battalion, under *SS-Hauptsturmführer* Jean Vermeire, was stationed in the Plowen/Locknitz region. *SS-Sturmbannführer* Jules Mathieu's reserve formations of soldiers who were unable to fight were stationed near Bergholz. More reservists were in Schmagerow and Bismarck – the combat reserves commanded by *SS-Obersturmführer* Marcel Bonniver.[18] Due to the chaotic nature of these last weeks of the war, the 69th Regiment of the *'Wallonien'* Division had been rebuilt, if in a rather complicated fashion. The regiment was comprised of about 900 men and the operational command was awarded to *SS-Sturmbannführer* Frans Hellebaut. They were divided into two battalions: the first commanded by *SS-Sturmbannführer* Derriks and the second

---

15   Delannoy means the reserve battalion under Jean Vermeire's command. The battalion comprised of all the elements unable to fight – the wounded, convalescents and the forced workers who had ended up in the *'Wallonien'* Division by accident.
16   Henri Derriks.
17   Delannoy, op. cit., p. 50.
18   Eddy de Bruyne's letter to the author from 14 March 2013.

67.   *SS-Obersturmbannführer* Conrad Schellong from the 27th *SS-Panzergrenadier* Volunteer Division *'Langemarck'*. (Author's own collection)

by Marcel Bonniver.[19]

At the time, *SS-Obersturmbannführer* Leon Degrelle was travelling a lot between Hanover and Berlin in order to keep himself up to speed on the changing events.[20]

On 15 April, the remaining Walloon and Flemish soldiers were assigned to *SS-Standartenführer* Thomas Müller – the commanding officer of the 27th *SS-Panzergrenadier* Division *'Langemarck'*. *SS-Obersturmbannführer* Conrad Schellong became the CO of this *Kampfgruppe*-turned-infantry.

On 17 April, the 69th Regiment of the *'Wallonien'* Division was divided. Derriks's group was deployed to Pomelen, while Bonniver's men were sent to Hohenholz. The two towns were located a couple of kilometres from the Oder's left bank. The battalions were to maintain readiness in case their intervention was needed.

The next evening, Derriks' *Kampfgruppe* left Schmagerow and reached Pomelen without incident, taking positions under fir trees on the dunes. Frans Hellebaut set his command post next to them. Bonniver's battalion took positions five kilometres to the west, near Hohenholz.[21]

---

19   de Bruyne, Rikmenspoel, op. cit., p. 296.
20   Devresse, op. cit., p. 1.
21   Ibid., p. 9.

Derriks's men set their camp in a little Pomelen forest. It was spring and they passed their time, lying under the trees, awaiting further developments. Meanwhile, the command staff tried to learn about the situation as much as they could. Given the expected counter-attack, Hellebaut scouted the terrain by the river. He was accompanied by Derriks and a couple of his officers. The positions around Huhnenberg were riddled with trenches. Light weapons were placed on concrete beds, with deep cover. It looked quite nice. At the foot of the cliff, 50 to 60 metres high, there was a wide beach, promising shelter from tactical fire. Below Huhnenberg, on the other side, there was a wide and completely exposed sand basin, spread all the way to the second level, two kilometres deep.[22]

On 20 April, the Soviets launched their attack, between the Kurów [Kurow] and Moczyły [Schillersdorf] villages. It was an easy operation given the scale of the deployed forces and means, as well as the obvious vulnerability of the enemy.

This is how Frans Hellebaut wrote about this event in his memoirs:

On 20 April, 5:30 AM, came an incredibly violent bombardment (two hundred and thirty-eight guns per kilometre) and destroyed the first echelon of our positions between Greifenhagen and Kurow. Thick fog kept the German artillery from launching a successful counter-attack and the 65th Red Army's assault troops easily crossed to the west bank of the river,[23] using cutters, ferries and motorboats, and suffered very few casualties. The soldiers, huddled in their trenches and bunkers, under dreadful fire, seemed not to notice anything. Finally, at 8:30 AM, the German commander found out that the first enemy elements might've already gained a beachhead at the foot of the first echelon, five kilometres between Kurow and Schillersdorf. The situation was so bad, that around 9 AM the Police Assault Brigade, threatened on both sides and fearing being written off, started to retreat. By leaving their positions in Huhnenberg,[24] they allowed the Russians to close in without much effort. The fog was dissipating slowly and the Soviet Air Force joined the action, bombarding the second echelon and cutting phone-lines, which paralysed the artillery and support troops alike.[25]

---

22 Ibid.
23 The 65th Army was a part of the 2nd Belorussian Front commanded by Marshal Konstantin Rokossovsky. In the middle of April, Rokossovsky had taken over the Oder front-line from the town Ognica near Schwedt to where the Oder joined the Baltic Sea. (ed.)
24 The town, which appears on the 1945 maps just above Kołbaskowo [Kolbitzow], currently does not exist.
25 Hellebaut, op. cit.

In these circumstances a new interim *Kampfgruppe* was created under the command of *SS-Sturmbannführer* Frans Hellebaut. He was assigned three battalions: the Flemish (*SS-Hauptsturmführer* Jean de Mulder), the Walloon (*SS-Sturmbannführer* Derriks) and the *'Kolberg'* Battalion. The *Kampfgruppe's* goals were made clear:

- 'De Mulder' Battalion retakes Huhnenberg
- 'Derriks' Battalion takes Rosówek [Neu-Rosow] and pushes back any enemy assaults[26]
- *'Kolberg'* Battalion does likewise in Kamieniec [Schöningen][27]

By then, *Kampfgruppe 'Derriks'* was the only fully battle-worthy Walloon unit and the only tactical formation in the entire *'Wallonien'* Division engaged in the fighting in April 1945. The group's CO was Henri Derriks and he had some 550 of the most battle-hardened volunteers, determined to stand to the very end.

Kampfgruppe 'Derriks's' complement (number two)[28] was as follows:[29]

Commanding Officer: *SS-Sturmbannführer* Henri Derriks

- 1st Company: *SS-Untersturmführer* Andre Regibeau (WIA 20/04/1945)
  - ◊ 1st Platoon: *SS-Untersturmführer* Daniel Wouters (KIA 20/04/1945)
  - ◊ 2nd Platoon: *SS-Untersturmführer* Jacques Leroy (WIA 20/04/1945)
  - ◊ 3rd Platoon: *SS-Hauptscharfuhrer* Maxime Havet (KIA 20/04/1945)
- 2nd Company: *SS-Untersturmführer* Mathieu de Coster (WIA 22/04/1945)
  - ◊ 1st Platoon: *SS-Untersturmführer* Jean Piron (WIA 20/04/1945), replaced by *SS-Oberscharführer* Raoul Roland
  - ◊ 2nd Platoon: *SS-Untersturmführer* Jose Gortz (KIA 21/04/1945)
  - ◊ 3rd Platoon: *SS-Untersturmführer* Roland Devresse
- 3rd Company: *SS-Obersturmführer* Leon Gillis
  - ◊ 1st Platoon: *SS-Obersturmführer* GePe (WIA 21 and 23/04/1945)
  - ◊ 2nd Platoon: *SS-Hauptscharfuhrer* Lucien Lambert
  - ◊ 3rd Platoon: *SS-Hauptscharfuhrer* Fidele Hendrickx
- 4th Company: *SS-Hauptscharfuhrer* Henri Thyssen (KIA 20/04/1945)

---

26 In literature, this formation is called either a *Kampfgruppe* or a battalion interchangeably.

27 de Bruyne, Rikmenspoel, op. cit., p. 296.

28 In earlier battles *Kampfgruppe 'Derriks'* had a very much different complement, which is why here the formation is designated as 'number two'.

29 de Bruyne, Rikmenspoel, op. cit., p. 298.

68.   *SS-Obersturmführer* Leon Gillis
with one of the men from his company
of which he had command until the
end of the Pomeranian Campaign.
(Michel le Roy's collection)

replaced by *SS-Untersturmführer* Monfils
◊   1st Platoon: *SS-Untersturmführer* Roger Gondry
◊   2nd Platoon: *SS-Untersturmführer* Charles Monfils
◊   3rd Platoon: *SS-Hauptscharfuhrer* Hector Landucci (KIA 23/04/1945)

On the afternoon of 20 April, Derriks had arrived in Rosówek and was immediately informed that the Soviet infantry was very close. Together with Frans Hellebaut, who came to inspect his troops, they chose to counter-attack. Leon Gillis's 3rd Company, so far unnoticed by the enemy, managed to take good firing positions. While Gillis and his men were busy trying to stop the Russians, the 1st Company (*SS-Untersturmführer* Regibeau) and the 2nd Company (*SS-Untersturmführer* de Coster) quickly reached the 3rd Company's forward positions. By following the 3rd, the 1st and 2nd, with the help of two platoons from the 4th Company, were able to take some 50 or 60 prisoners. The Burgundians won the first round. The enemy, surprised by the sudden counter-attack, lost their footing and retreated to the dunes of Moczyły. Both companies, still following the 3rd with the two platoons from the 4th, kept advancing.

69.   The Walloon volunteer *SS-Grenadier* Henri Lanin. This photograph was taken during the Burgundians' operations on Western Pomerania; other details remain unknown. (Michel le Roy's collection)

At around 2:00 p.m. things seemed relatively calm. Frans Hellebaut:

The situation was under control and we had a wide view of the entire sector from our dunes. Impressive squadrons of enemy bombers were circling the sky. Their patrols, several fighter planes each, kept targeting the *Flak* battery, as well as anything else they could. To the north, Kolbitzow was ablaze, but the Russians, who had taken Huhnenberg some distance away, didn't show any activity.[30]

The euphoria was short-lived, however, because the Soviet artillery commenced fire on the Walloon positions, forcing them to dig in. Enemy fighters, flying low above the ground, joined in the action, too. At around 4:45 p.m., having covered about two kilometres of ground, the 1st Company reached the suburbs of Moczyły, but they had lost communication with the 2nd Company in their fervour. In any case, the Oder's bank was just 500 metres ahead![31]

The temptation to reach the river was just too good to pass up! Regibeau

---

30 Hellebaut, op. cit.
31 de Bruyne, Rikmenspoel, op. cit., p. 298.

70. *SS-Untersturmführer* Daniel Wouters as an *SS-Sturmmann*. The photograph was taken in July 1943. (Michel le Roy's collection)

and his men renewed their attack bravely, but at a heavy price. The Russians took positions on the upper floors of several buildings and their machine gun fire forced the Walloons to stop. The Soviet counter-attack may not have been successful, but the Walloon officers and NCOs kept falling one by one to the sniper's bullet. Maxime Havet was killed, *SS-Untersturmführer* Jacques Leroy and *SS-Scharführer* Georges Piessevaux were wounded. Regibeau, trying to take their place, kept running from bush to bush, encouraging his boys and helping to carry the most badly wounded back to the rear. Suddenly, he fell, as if struck by lightning – he was seriously injured in both thighs. That was his third injury in the last six weeks and the eighth since he had come to the Eastern Front. The 1st Platoon's leader, 21-year-old *SS-Untersturmführer* Daniel Wouters, took command of the 1st Company.[32]

Meanwhile, *SS-Obersturmführer* Gillis's 3rd Company received reinforcements from a platoon from the 4th, led by *SS-Hauptscharführer* Hector Landucci. They moved forward to fill the gap between the 1st and 2nd. Unfortunately, they failed. Thyssen, who had been promoted to *SS-Hauptsturmführer* earlier that day, volunteered to liaise with the remnants of the

---

32 Ibid.

71. Jose Gortz prior to enlistment.
(Eddy de Bruyne's collection)

1st Company. A short while later, he was killed by a sniper.

The situation of the right flank was no better: the weakening 2nd Company was halted on their way to Kamieniec and the leader of the 3rd Platoon, *SS-Untersturmführer* Jose Gortz, had fallen. The Walloons still had 800 metres of open terrain between them and the enemy. *SS-Untersturmführer* Roland Devresse's platoon volunteered to push the Russians out of the dunes down the Oder. Despite their valiant efforts, their mission was a failure and Devresse and his men got pinned down south of Moczyły.[33]

At around 5:00 p.m., the Assault Battalion *'Kolberg'* arrived, bringing a company of tank hunters and seven cannons. They attacked from the riverside dunes, towards Moczyły, and managed to get the Walloon companies out of the fix they were in. The Soviets, however, were quick to react and the 3rd Company, despite the support of their friends from the *Wehrmacht*, was definitively stopped.[34]

General Hasso von Manteuffel was, however, determined to continue the assault and late in the afternoon, on 20 April 1945, he sent the three dwindling battalions from the 27th *SS*-Volunteer Grenadier Division *'Langemarck'* to the

33 Ibid.
34 Ibid.

72. Jose Gortz in *Waffen-SS* uniform.
He was killed in action on 21 April
1945 near Kamieniec [Schöningen].
(Michel le Roy's collection)

Kamieniec [Schöningen] – Gryfino [Greifenhagen] area.

In the meantime, the Walloons were preparing to cross to their battle-stations under the cover of the night. Further to the north, during nightly battle with the Russians, they were pushed back to the Oder's banks. The result was that the German command ordered the *Kampfgruppe 'Langemarck's'* CO, *SS-Obersturmbannführer* Conrad Schellong, to reclaim Huhnenberg.[35]

The task of coordinating the Walloon-Flemish-German movements was assigned to *SS-Sturmbannführer* Hellebaut. The attack was scheduled at 4:00 a.m. on 21 April 1945 and was to be accompanied by the usual artillery preparations, which, instead of two hours, lasted barely 10 minutes. Leon Degrelle, in his book *Eastern Front* speaks of those moments on the Oder's left bank:

> Even in Stargard, two months previously, we had but six, ten shells a day for one cannon. Before that last battle over Oder, our orders were even worse: our fire was limited to one shell per barrel daily. One shell. Just one! Limits for our mortars were almost just as bad: two shots per day (...) In reality: zero.[36]

Kampfgruppe 'Derriks' was ordered to attack towards Moczyły. The companies

---

35 de Bruyne, Rikmenspoel, op. cit., p. 299.
36 Degrelle, op. cit., p. 343.

73.   *SS-Untersturmführer* Roger
Gondry – a leader of one of the platoons
in *Kampfgruppe 'Derriks'* – during the
final stages of the formation's operations.
(Michel le Roy's collection)

taking part in the assault were as follows:

- 3rd Company with some 30 survivors from the 1st Company and with *SS-Hauptscharführer* Landucci's platoon on the left flank
- 2nd Company with *SS-Untersturmführer* Gondry's platoon on the right
- Support of some five tanks and elements from the 4th Company

SS-Obersturmführer Leon Gillis quickly came under heavy fire from the enemy's artillery and had to stop his advance after only a hundred metres. *SS-Untersturmführer* de Coster's company, despite intense shelling, was able to move a little deeper, but when they finally reached the Russian lines, they had only 15 men left! After nightfall they retreated to their former positions, taking their wounded and burying their dead.

As the dawn approached, it became clear that the assault was a complete fiasco and communication with the Flemish battalion on the left and *'Kolberg'* Battalion on the right had been lost. The brunt of the Soviet attack came in the late afternoon hours from the north, threatening Kołbaskowo [Kolbitzow] and Rosówek. *SS-Sturmbannführer* Hellebaut was forced to move the Walloons (reduced to some 130 men, more or less ready to fight) back to their positions near Rosówek from the day before. During the night, Derriks and his men crossed the

Berlin – Gdańsk [Danzig] highway and reached Pomelen, away from the main front-line.

Having spent the night in Pomelen did not lift the soldiers' spirits much. On the morning of 22 April, Henri Derriks was trying to regroup his thinning battalion. The command was decimated, their numbers barely the size of a company. The survivors suffered greatly, standing at the assembly and seeing so many of their friends were missing. Roland Devresse had only some 10 men left in his platoon and still he could have considered himself a lucky man, since other platoons ceased to exist altogether. GePe, ever the optimist, saw things in a relatively good perspective. It would be worth to hear from him, especially because he provided a lot of details, which, in a way, breathe life into those difficult moments.[37]

In early morning, 22 April, after ablutions and a tasty meal, we go back to our daily business. I'm trying to fix a star on my epaulettes and the bars on my collar.[38] It's the rule, the tradition, the sense of propriety, each time a promotion happens. I go to Major Hellebaut's command post. I open the door and ... I remember this, as if it had happened yesterday.[39]

Devresse claims GePe was lucky to remember everything so well. He was surprised at this special attention to symbols in such a moment, which he expresses in this nostalgia-filled comment: ' ... to fix a star, present himself to the major – what style ... while we live in an absurd world that is falling apart, surrounded by our dead, awaiting our return to the front-line for the last time, I'm sure ... '[40]

And GePe again:

Several minutes later we found ourselves in front of his[41] command post, on the street. Gillis joined us and we talked a little. On the corner of the street, a trap pulled by a horse showed up. Gillis told us who the carter was: he was a duty officer from the 4th Company, Thyssen's aide. Inside the trap we found a coffin or, rather, something that was supposed to be a coffin. Oh yes, this brave adjutant, crazy by pain and loss, managed to recover the body of his

---

37 Devresse, op. cit., p. 26.
38 GePe means his promotion to *SS-Obersturmführer*.
39 GePe, *En Poméranie Coule l'Oder*.
40 Devresse, op. cit., p. 26.
41 *SS-Sturmbannführer* Frans Hellebaut's.

dear captain, our friend, Henri Thyssen. God only knows how the hand-over happened. He found a couple of boards somewhere and fixed up a coffin. He passed us by, not even granting us a glance, completely focused on his task: to honour his last road. Major Hellebaut, always so very great-century-style, boomed: 'The fallen belong to the battlefield! Filled with them, it goes on, unwavering.' Gillis and I, filled with deep respect for our great friend, who moved on before us ... [42]

Under the cover of the Pomelen woods, the Burgundians were preparing to return to the front-line, without a shred of joy, with a fatalistic attitude, but with one thought in mind: 'Volunteers we are, volunteers we will be 'till the end!'.[43]

SS-Obersturmführer GePe expresses the same belief, if with a little more lyricism:

The orders keep coming always the same. Stand your ground. To an army at the front-line it's just a matter of life. What orders? It's simple: you go back, you go in. As said before, nothing can scare us more. Nothing will ever seem more tragic, terrible and shocking. That's just impossible! We know. But we go back and back, and it never gives us any euphoria any more. If we could, we would have chosen different skies, more merciful. As it is, our fate is to obey, keep faith and follow orders. And so we go again ... on that road so very familiar ... [44]

On 22 April, the merciless and bitter battle over the Oder lasted the entire day. The troops of the *'Langemarck'* and *'Wallonien'* divisions, which existed only on paper by now, were mixed up, defending themselves ever so desperately. Around noon, two thinned Walloon companies clashed with the Soviet forces by Rosówek dunes. One of the platoons from the 2nd Company, under *SS-Obersturmführer* Graff, had been sent there to reinforce the weakening defenders and got caught up in a fierce battle, suffering heavy casualties.

Roland Devresse remember this episode:

In reality we simply returned to our old route from 20 April. Big difference! Howling emptiness in our ranks. Three-fourths of our comrades are gone! We cross the highway in small groups, the Soviet Air Force is everywhere. We

---

42 GePe, op. cit.
43 Devresse, op. cit., p. 26.
44 GePe, op. cit.

74. *SS-Hauptscharfuhrer* Hector Landucci – one of the volunteers who participated in the counter-attack near Rosówek [Neu-Rosow] on 23 April 1945 and who had fallen on the same day. (Michel le Roy's collection)

take back our positions on the Neu-Rosow dunes, which we had left behind in previous days. Derriks was back at Schellong's command post, a couple of hundreds kilometres away.[45]

Frans Hellebaut adds a few words as well:

Around noon, Derriks had returned to take the Neu-Rosow dunes and he brought the rest of his battalion regrouped into two riflemen companies. Still in shock after having lost so many friends, they were supposed to be reinforced by one of the companies from Bonniver's battalion. They were waiting in vain, though. The troops had to move back to the road towards Neu-Rosow, further south, to stop the advance of enemy tanks, appearing out of the neighbouring sector.[46]

Soviet activity in the sector in question had stopped during the night. Conrad Schellong allowed Henri Derriks's exhausted survivors to retreat to Pomelen and rest for a while. They were replaced by 20 men, who were to form

---

45 Devresse, op. cit., p. 27.
46 Hellebaut, op. cit.

a kind of rearguard and to take the positions abandoned by the core of the *Kampfgruppe*. Every one of those men had volunteered. The complement of this tiny rearguard was as follows: *SS-Obersturmführer* GePe, *SS-Untersturmführer* Albert Verpoorten, Jean Hallebardier, Roland Devresse, Roger Gondry, *SS-Hauptscharführer* Hector Landucci, *SS-Scharführer* Bayard and van Malderen – and 12 privates.[47] This fact is confirmed by Frans Hellebaut in a rather official and succinct tone:

> After nightfall the sector was quiet. Schellong finally allowed Derriks to send his men, shivering from the cold, back to Pomelen. As far as I know, twenty of them stayed back until watch-change ... the volunteers were quickly discovered: lieutenants GePe, Verpoorten and Hallebardier, platoon leaders Gondry, Devresse and Landucci, sergeants Bayard and van Malderen and twelve Legionnaires had spent the rest of the night under the sky, bothered by no one.[48]

GePe tells the story of the difficulties he had choosing those 12 desperate men. Finally, he decided that in these circumstances, when they were short on company commanders, most of whom were killed or otherwise gone, he would remain with the rest of the officers present. These volunteers could serve as a symbol of their final resistance against the Red Army in the last days of the Second World War:

'I do remember how these twenty men were received into the ranks. To them everything went smoothly, easily. I thought different. To me it was hard and slow. But hard or easy, that's a meaningless detail'.[49]

One of those 'twenty', Roland Devresse elaborates:

> The recruitment of the twenty volunteers for that last bastion of honour couldn't be anything but difficult. We had to convince a couple of good guys, tired and spent, to make the sacrifice, allowing their friends their ignominious retreat. And that was a great sacrifice to ask for! Twenty volunteers had vowed not to abandon the 'battalion'. I could see the lowered heads and worried looks. I went to de Coster's[50] command post for instruction, which was located in a small bunker burrowed in a dune slope. I found him lying in a corner. He had been

---

47 de Bruyne, Rikmenspoel, op. cit., p. 300.
48 Hellebaut, op. cit.
49 GePe, op. cit.
50 *SS-Untersturmführer* Mathieu de Coster, 2nd Company commander in *Kampfgruppe 'Derriks'*.

75.   *SS-Untersturmführer* Albert Verpoorten – another one of the 20 Burgundians
who had fought in Rosówek [Neu-Rosow]. (Charles Verpoorten's collection)

wounded the previous day and his brother had died during the first counter-
attack, which excused his somewhat worsened psychological condition and I
could understand him perfectly. I had already made my decision and told him
I would represent the 2nd Company among the volunteers, hoping I would
be able to find a couple of men with whom I would be able to form a small
but capable defence team. He thanked me, shaking my hand sincerely. I may
not have been a particularly talented recruiter, but I did find two brave boys, a
sergeant and a corporal, who were ready to face new adventure. The three of us
were to represent the 2nd Company.

The 'battalion' is getting ready to go back to the Pomelen highway, just
like they did last night. The volunteers are regrouping and I am happy to see
my old friends from the youth organisation: Gondry and Landucci. Young
Burgundians will be well represented in that battle for honour.[51]

Devresse also speaks well of his CO, *SS-Sturmbannführer* Henri Derriks:

---

51   Devresse, op. cit., p. 27.

76.   Fields near Rosówek [Neu-Rosow]. In exactly this kind of open terrain, the
Walloons had to fight; here is a modern view. (Charles Verpoorten's collection)

Derriks had come to see our boys off and he turned to us respectfully. We will
be his last barricade and he is aware that this time very few will go back with
him! He was the one who had negotiated that strange deal with Schellong:
twenty really determined guys for a hundred broken. Derriks was the right
man in the right place. The atmosphere at the command post, considering the
crisis of the past few days, was rich with alcohol, which suited Derriks, who
always knew how to choose an opportune moment to annul a bad decision
made by his commander and drinking buddy – Schellong. In July of 1945, me
and Gondry were close to Derriks in an English POW camp for officers and he
would tell us his secrets of those dark times. In the meantime, in that same way
known only to him, he had negotiated our final retreat, which was why four of
the survivors of that slaughter still owe him their lives.[52]

The group of volunteers took positions on the slope of the dune in Rosówek.
As he was the ranking officer, GePe took command. According to Roland
Devresse, however, the entire 20 was just one group of warriors and rank didn't
matter – and everybody just did what they had to and without actually waiting

---

52   Ibid., p. 28.

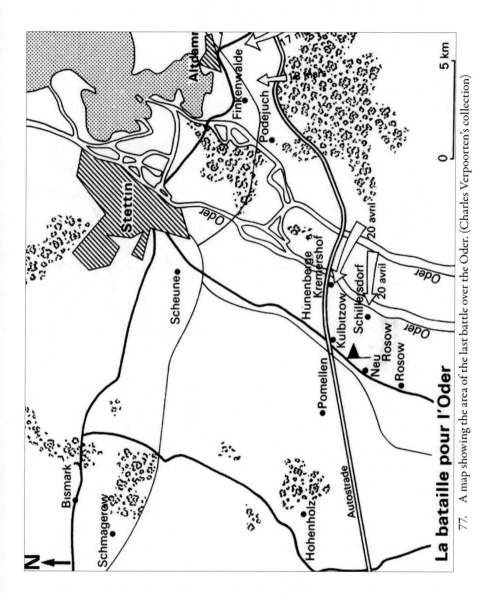

77. A map showing the area of the last battle over the Oder. (Charles Verpoorten's collection)

for orders, too. They were a desperate bunch, choosing the best solutions based on instinct, determined to fight to the last. In the morning, the little group was assigned to the local command.[53]

GePe does not remember the incident fondly:

We went back to the same road as yesterday, marching down the dune range, all the way to Rosówek [Neu-Rosow]. The little town will have to stay in my memory, for sure. The order was clear: go and report to the captain leading the defence. I saw the last house, went down to the basement and found him there, sitting by a small table, next to a radio.

'Your men, huh? They holding or fucking around?' he asked impudently.

'*Hauptsturmführer*, I take offence at this!' I said and added, 'What are your orders?'

'Reinforce positions in front of the town,' he said.

'We will go there. And I invite you to come as well, if you want to find an answer to your question!'

The boor, the bastard, who does he think he is? These were the thoughts running through my head.[54]

Roland Devresse also describes the last hours before enemy assault:

Our arrival at the defensive positions in Neu-Rosow was orderly and as discreet as possible. Luckily, some real tactical trenches were still there, as well as some communication ditches. As for the men already there, we had to look for them: several pitiful shooters had dug in in their foxholes, a little way behind the *Flak* cannon, which was nearby. I also think there was one or two Pak75s there, which were supposed to spot the T-34s coming from ahead. In complete silence twenty men took control of fifty square metres of space, including trenches, keeping eye contact with each other. This diverse group of soldiers was infused by a sense of unity and common goal. The weather was much better now and the skies above were clear and the plain was very visible. Leaning against the slope of the embankment, I tried to locate enemy positions. From afar I could see brown shapes moving from time to time. I was worried that these dark masses were hiding, firing their guns at us from a distance. They were using the tanks as artillery in direct fire ... for now. We had to hide deep in our foxholes. All

---

53 Ibid., p. 29.
54 GePe, op. cit.

78.   A building at the rear of Rosówek [Neu-Rosow] serving as a field hospital during the battle on 23 April 1945. (Charles Verpoorten's collection)

over the field, their grenades sprung into action and I will have you know that the Russians were masters at wielding this particular weapon. With perfect visibility, they were able to locate every one-man trench and eliminate it. I wasn't using my machine gun, because it'd be a waste of ammo at this range and I had only two magazines left. In other words, that's just how it is sometimes in war, that we let the bad guys shoot over our heads, unable to retaliate, but still hoping to get lucky.[55]

Since dawn, 23 April, these 20 men tried all they could to stop the Soviet infantry from infiltrating Rosówek. In a matter of hours of bitter battle, 10 of the Burgundians had been killed or badly wounded. Hector Landucci died around 3:00 p.m. Moments later, a grenade or an artillery shell had exploded in the hole GePe, Verpoorten and two other communications officers had been hiding in. The liaison officers were killed instantly and Verpoorten was fatally injured.[56]

GePe, despite serious wounds, had lived. He is also the one to tell us a little bit more about this tragic episode:

---

55   Devresse, op. cit., p. 29-30.
56   A different take on Albert Verpoorten's fate can be found in Appendix II.

This is getting bad. I took position (such a beautiful word!) on the right wing to support the arriving back-up, as well as couriers heading for Derriks's command post. In a small crater carved by shell and bomb, there were three of us: Verpoorten, the boys I chose to accompany me as couriers[57] if need be, and myself. The steady fire renewed. It ploughed through every metre of the terrain. Six or seven of our men already had been eliminated from the fight, wounded. I could only try to lift their spirits as they passed me by, heading for Major Derriks's command post. Suddenly, a metallic sound rang on my left. Could that be shrapnel, razor-sharp and hot as flames? I had no time to check, 'cause a young boy with a round doll-like face, red all over, ran up and plunged into my trench, legs first, yelling, 'Lieutenant, Adjutant Landucci's been killed!' At the same time, as he was mid-sentence, something exploded in my foxhole, a grenade or a shell. There was a shrill in my ears, piercing and sharp. My face leaning on the wall of the foxhole, I kept muttering, 'Such beautiful death you had!'

The real horror of these terrible moments rings in Roland Devresse's words also:

For some time now, we've been haunted by fire from two directions, Russian mortars have us good and keep shooting, 'till we're gone. Our defeat is certain, we don't even dare to raise our heads, huddled in our foxholes, we wait for the end of the storm. We're doomed, the target-practice is getting worse. Gondry yelled from his hole that Landucci had been fatally wounded. A strike smack in the middle of Paquot's trench kills Verpoorten and injures a courier, who doubled back in pain. He had left a description of the event, full of pathos, telling of a Walloon lieutenant being held up by a Flemish soldier who was encouraging him to live and helping him get to Derriks's command post, and then going back. Our lines are emptying fast. I feel an overwhelming need to speak to someone ... At that exact moment Gondry, having left his position, jumps down into my foxhole. I was relieved and we held each other up like lost children. He had told me of Landucci's death, an edge to his voice. They were good friends since 10 March 1942. We think this is the end of all. But we push back the doubt and get back to our watch. The Russians are still holding back their assault. We see them circling, ever so bolder. Their tanks move up a little,

---

57 GePe, op. cit.

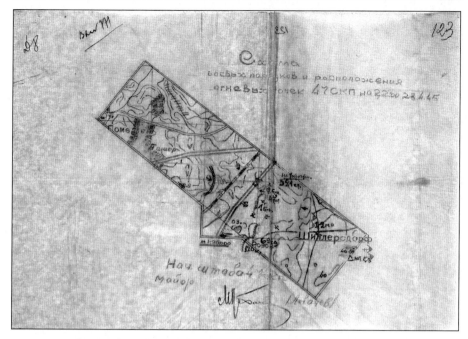

79. A drawing from the Soviet archives representing the positions of the Red Army forces before the attack on Rosówek [Neu-Rosow]. (Charles Verpoorten's collection)

still seemingly unwilling to strike, though. If they wanted, they'd be on us in moments and we'd be dead in a split of a second. Our only Pak gun left is still in its position but it's almost out of ammo. It'd be traced and destroyed if it tried to fire.[58]

Leon Degrelle mentions Verpoorten's death as well: 'Lieutenant Albert Verpoorten, that young writer, so full of energy and humour, fell dead, his chest ripped wide open and his arms torn apart. On that tragic day, 21 April 1945, six times had the Walloons received an order to renew their assault. And six times they had thrown themselves into the thick of battle'.[59]

At 4:00 p.m., only four Burgundians were left to defend their positions: Gondry, Devresse, van Malderen and Quinaud. The rest had been killed or wounded. A short while later, the remaining survivors received orders to return to one of the weakened Walloon companies.[60]

58 Devresse, op. cit., p. 31.
59 Eddy de Bruyne and Charles Verpoorten give a different date – 23 April 1945 – and this is the date we should see as the most reliable.
60 de Bruyne, Rikmenspoel, op. cit., p. 300.

80.   A building in Rosówek [Neu-Rosow] – a likely site of Henri Derriks's command
post. This photograph was taken in October 2008. (Charles Verpoorten's collection)

Once again, we shall return to Roland Devresse's unique recollections. He was one of the few Walloons who had survived the storm that fell on the left banks of the Oder at the end of April 1945:

> What will the last footmen do, then? How many are there left? A few Germans on our right, a few Flemish on our left, a little further back on our second line, and the last Burgundian company whose complement I cannot account for. Given the known numbers of the dead and wounded who had, to my knowledge, been evacuated, there couldn't be left more than twenty from our original count. The last blow to the morale: suddenly, I saw a sergeant emerge from his trench, the Eastern Front Medal and the Iron Cross, 1st Class on his chest. He ran to the rear in fear. He didn't seem wounded; he just couldn't take it anymore. That could happen to the best of us in circumstances like these! This time I realised it truly was the end!
>
> Yet, a miracle happened. [The] Last of Derriks's couriers had slipped to our positions and he yelled to us, waving his hands. Turned out he had our orders to retreat! Those still alive, left their trenches and, stumbling, headed for the command post, some couple hundred metres away, I think. Stupidly, we took a head-count ... there was four of us!
>
> Derriks came out to meet us. We could feel he'd be glad to hug us but he

just ordered dryly, 'Hurry up before I change my mind!' We realised he had just returned from the commander of the entire front-line, Schellong, having managed to tear the last of us from the massacre as sure as it was unnecessary. We moved like automatons, Roger Gondry with one of his men and myself, my sergeant from the 2nd Company at my side. This was a war blessing, indeed!

We followed, side by side, as Derriks left the front-line with four of his men ... four men! At a turn of the road, we found a well-camouflaged car with a radio station. A couple of Germans milled about, listening to the latest news. Fighting in Berlin, *Führer* and his men in battle. The Americans were close, but they will fight the Russians along with us. The Americans assaulting! We didn't believe it too much, that would just be too good! We're going to march through the night, looking for the rest of our battalion. Only at sunset will we reach our quarters, though. Everybody kept looking at us as if we were ghosts, as if they had already decided we were dead.[61]

The great sacrifice of the volunteers from *Kampfgruppe 'Derriks'* quickly echoed throughout other Walloon formations, even those not directly involved in the action; whose COs were doing everything to keep up the morale, which was waning in the everlasting retreat. Things were not much better in the 7th Company of the 2nd Battalion, commanded by *SS-Hauptsturmführer* Marcel Bonniver.

One of the soldiers of that company, Freddy Jacques, describes Leon Degrelle's visit and the impact the Walloon *Volksführer's* speech had on him and his comrades:

Relaxed, I joined Lieutenant Graff's 7th Company. For a couple of days we held the third defensive line around Bergholz. Modest[62] kept giving speech after speech. Sometime after the 20 April, we were waiting for him at 6 PM. Remembering the good old traditions, he arrived at 8, dirty and muddied. He got right to the point:

'Comrades, firstly, please forgive me my tardiness. I was held up with Derriks's battalion which has been covering itself with glory since morning. At dawn, the Russians had crossed the Oder, gaining a large bridgehead. Derriks's

61 Devresse, op. cit., p. 32.
62 Leon Degrelle's unofficial nickname. The soldiers called him that – surprised by his modesty when he joined the Walloon Legion as a private. They humorously nicknamed him 'Modest the First, Prince of Burgundy'.

81.   *SS-Untersturmführer* Jean Hallebardier
– a recipient of the Knight's Cross (presented
with the award on 20 April 1945), he was
wounded during the sacrifice of Rosówek [Neu-
Rosow]. He survived the war and was sentenced
to prison for collaboration; his subsequent fate
remains unknown. (Michel le Roy's collection)

battalion reacted swiftly and launched a counter-attack. With glorious
enthusiasm, they pushed the Russians back seven kilometres and now they are a
couple of hundred metres from the river, awaiting reinforcements to completely
annihilate the enemy bridgehead. Comrades, these are dangerous times, the
Russians are giving everything they've got in this last assault. We are lucky (!)
to have found ourselves at this pivotal point of this gigantic battle.'

Then he went on, on his favourite subject, and we kept listening, as was
appropriate. Our ears were practically falling off from his ever so numerously
and frequently repeated bullshit: civilisation, heritage, etc. What was
interesting, however, was that he finally hinted that our Motherland was lost –
it didn't take a genius strategist to know that! – but we had to continue our fight
to the death so that the Americans could reach the Oder. We cannot save our
country but, still, it was all that mattered. On our part, we did everything we
could to save Belgium in the face of German victory! So we did our duty! Long
live Belgium! Finally, Modest, in a great burst of 'clairvoyance' said, 'When you
return, you'll be in no danger, they'll be satisfied with having me!'

Alas, that turned out not to be the case but I didn't realise that until much
later.[63]

---

63 Jacques, op. cit.

82.   Two soldiers of the '*Wallonien*' Division somewhere on the Eastern Front. (Charles Verpoorten's collection)

The infantry-sized *Kampfgruppe 'Schellong'*, which included the Walloons, had been dismantled due to inadequate battle-worthiness caused by loss of the majority of its complement. The last Walloon troops joined the reserve battalion of their mother-formation around Bergholz. On 24 April, all Burgundians had been regrouped to the Brussow-Wollshow sector and sent to the rear of the front behind the River Ucker, north of Prenzlau.

9

End of the Line

While the non-line Walloon troops marched west to avoid Soviet prison camps and to surrender to the Americans, the last miserable remnants of the two battalions from the 69th Regiment of the 28th SS-Volunteer Grenadier Division *'Wallonien'* engaged in battle one last time. Their mission was to defend three towns: Bandelow, Trebenow and Schönwerder-Ellinen.

At the turn of 26/27 April, Prenzlau came under attack by Russian armoured troops who had reached the western suburbs. The 2nd Battalion of the 69th Regiment, commanded by *SS-Hauptsturmführer* Marcel Bonniver, had been defending the village of Schönwerder for the last couple of hours. Around midnight, a group of Russian tanks showed up on the road connecting Prenzlau and Neubrandenburg. They were stopped, however, by hastily-built anti-tank ditches. In the afternoon, the Russian infantry assaulted Schönwerder from the south and east. Exploiting the *Wehrmacht* Company's weakness, the Soviets managed to take the village.

Two Walloon platoons counter-attacked immediately and were locked in battle for every single building. In close quarters combat, *SS-Untersturmführer* Count de Backer de Reville received fatal wounds. A bunch of volunteers carved their way with grenades but proved to be ultimately helpless against Soviet artillery and rockets.

Once more we shall quote Abel Delannoy, who thus describes the fighting around Schönwerder:

> The Soviets crossed the Oder on 20 April. Our *Kampfgruppe* and *'Langemarck'* Battalion countered and stalled their attack. Not for long though and at a heavy price! How many veterans of the Eastern Front did not come back! I still think of one of them, commandant Henri 'Bolshoi' Thyssen[1] from the 4th Company, a very nice Burgundian whom everybody loved. On parades, given his short stature, he would proudly carry our banner with the Burgundian

---

1   *SS-Hauptsturmführer* fell in battle on 20 April 1945.

83.   A photograph of a parade in the middle of 1944, which took place in the Belgian town of Charleroi. In the middle is *SS-Obersturmführer* Henri Thyssen, who was killed in action on 20 April 1945 near Moczyły [Schillersdorf]. (J.L. Roba's collection)

Cross[2] and the motto: 'He who attacks it, get stung'. The second of Captain Bonniver's battalions arrived on 27 April on the side flank of the Reds, who were marching down the Szczecin – Berlin highway.

As we were leaving the town, we got our orders. The commander had sent us on a run-down road so that we may move from the front towards a church the Reds had taken. They had a great vantage point on that bell-tower and we were an easy target on this open terrain. We were stopped by a hail of bullets. I screamed an order for steady retreat. In such moments as these, a hero or not, when hundreds of bullets whizz by your ears like furious wasps, you always feel a powerful pressure in your stomach. It's a great moment, actually, to remember all the good reasons you should not fall apart: you're a volunteer, after all, a Burgundian and an officer. It's not like in the movies where there are officers,

---

2   In heraldry, it was a variation on the isosceles spiked cross of St Andrew. The Walloon Legion used a red cross on a white background. The Burgundian Cross had been in use on since 1408, when it appeared on the banners of the Prince of Burgundy. In later times it appeared in Spanish and Dutch heraldry, used by those who believed themselves to be the true and moral heirs to the Burgundian State. (ed.)

stuffed into their immaculate uniforms, with their beautifully shiny boots and their kepi roguishly pulled over their ears, a pretty gun all the weapon they need! We go back to the Schönwerder exit for new orders: we need to launch an attack on that church, using the nearby houses for cover. The captain warned me honestly that already two platoons had tried and the CO of one of them got killed and the other – grievously wounded. It didn't sound promising at all.

And so we tried to the take the church in Schönwerder! At that very moment, the katyusha fire had reduced my platoon to dust. A huge wall had fallen before me, exploding red. Lieutenant G fell on my right, his arms spread wide. An ominous growl announced the second shell coming. I found myself in a shallow trench with other Burgundians. We had only one shovel. I started digging with my bare hands. Better this than nothing.[3]

At around 6:00 p.m. the Walloons were allowed to fall back.

Leon Degrelle visited his men for the last time on the 24 April 1945, supervising the last supply intake and presiding over an award ceremony, many of which had been posthumous.

He had remained in the area of combat until 28 April 1945. The day before he had ordered one of his aides to secure a mysterious heavy box, the contents of which remains a secret until this day. Soon thereafter he left the Castle Zahren but not before *SS-Sturmbannführer* Frans Hellebaut had. Degrelle was accompanied by Charles Generet, Robert Duwelz, Hahn and Jules Sandron, an *SS-Untersturmführer* from the I/69[4] whom *SS-Sturmbannführer* Jules Mathieu had assigned to the division in order to help coordinate Hahn's activities in the command office. Degrelle's entourage also included Florent Emsix and Guillaume 'Willy' Graide, as well as two drivers. *SS-Obersturmführer* Emsix and Graide had left the group the next day, on 29 April. Only *SS-Sturmbannführer* Jules Mathieu was missing from the fellowship. His boss did ask him to come but given the choice between helping a friend and doing his duty, Mathieu had chosen the latter. He just couldn't leave his men behind.[5]

The Walloon troops were completely bled out at this point and on 28 April they were assigned to the III SS Corps (Germanic) as tactical reserve and commenced a five-day retreat march towards Schwerin via Woddeck, Neubrandenburg, Zahren, Stavenhagen, Nahin, Damero, Klein Poserin and Krivitz.

---

3   Delannoy, Abel, *Confession d'un SS*, pp. 51-52.
4   1st Battalion of the 69th Regiment in the *'Wallonien'* Division.
5   de Bruyne, Eddy, *Leon Degrelle et la Legion Wallonie...* (Liege, 2011), p. 248.

Richard Landwehr, in his aforementioned book *The Wallonien*, expresses an interesting view on this final chapter of the Walloon *SS* division. Namely, he believes that on 30 April 1945, in a village called Nossentiner Hutte, there was the first and last briefing of the commanding officers of the three volunteer formations: 'Charlemagne', 'Langemarck' and 'Wallonien'. The 'Wallonien's' last odyssey allegedly took place in Denmark where the remnants of the most seasoned and tested volunteers (some 800 men) were forced to capitulate.[6]

A more believable version of events can be found in a letter written to the author by the Belgian historian Eddy de Bruyne. De Bruyne claims that documents he had seen suggested that the only participants of the meeting had been Leon Degrelle and *SS-Standartenführer* Thomas Müller, the commander of the Flemish *SS-Divisiongruppe*[7] 'Müller'[8] *created on 15 April 1945. A similar account can be found in Das Ende Zwischen Oder un Elbe – Der Kampf um Berlin 1945* by Wilhelm Tieke. The talks concerned the end of the fighting and how to re-establish communications between troops.

Meanwhile, the Walloon Legion's archives had already fallen into Russian hands even though Degrelle had ordered them to be saved at all costs. *SS-Sturmbannführer* Jacobs, who had been tasked with the mission, was unable to complete it, despite his most sincere efforts. He did, however, manage to secure his commander's political manifesto which had been entrusted to him on 14 March 1945 in Szczecin.[9] As for the capitulation of the Walloon volunteers in Denmark, we can consider this hypothesis to be an absolute myth. Degrelle only expressed his desire to regroup through the Danish border but he was aware that that was an impossibility. We can suppose then that this was the reason he had issued clean certificates for foreign industry workers to all his men, which was to help them avoid Belgian justice. During a meeting between Degrelle and *SS-Reichsführer* Heinrich Himmler, which took place on 2 May 1945 in Lubeck, when asked how many men did he bring, Degrelle said 'Two'. Their names were Generet and Duwelz. The third Walloon, a driver, had been demobilised previously.[10]

On 1 May 1945, the American Army had reached Lubeck and Schwerin. At around 1:00 p.m., by terms of a local cease-fire, the Allies entered Hamburg.

---

6   Landwehr, Richard, *The Wallonien – The History of...* (Bennington, 2006), p. 45.
7   A division group was a common sight in the last phase of the war. It was a German provisional unit created from the remnants of a division or founded on the basis of a division staff. Aside from line battalions, it usually had some vestigial division units. (ed.)
8   Eddy de Bruyne's letter to the author from 20 March 2013.
9   de Bruyne, op. cit., p. 250.
10   Eddy de Bruyne's letter to the author from 20 March 2013.

On the same day, *SS-Untersturmführer* Albert Steiver had given Henri Derriks and Frans Hellebaut a sealed letter written by Leon Degrelle. The letter read as follows:

> To majors Hellebaut and Derriks,
>
> To captain Bonivert (resic).
>
> I'm going to see the RFSS[11] in Lubeck to talk about truce.
>
> I doubt a sudden cease-fire would stop all our men in place. It would be good for all of them to come to the Lubeck sector as soon as possible, too. The official order is to move out in groups immediately, by all means, on trucks going to the rendezvous site in Lubeck. It would be better and safer for our men to hitch-hike instead of increasing movements which would get the Legion caught by the Russians.
>
> I also attach worker slips. I will join the meeting in Lubeck to discuss truce. I will send a delegation to the Americans. You can count on me.
>
> (se) L. Degrelle.[12]

SS-Untersturmführer Steiver was unable to find *SS-Sturmbannführer* Hellebaut. He gave the letter to *SS-Sturmbannführer* Derriks. A second message, also delivered by Steiver, included an order to go to Bad-Segeberg, then to Lubeck and then to Denmark. In full battle gear they were to join the Northern Front.

On 1 March 1945, Degrelle and company had spent the night in Kalkhorst. Himmler had passed through there on the morning of the 2nd. Degrelle did not have the chance to see him, though. Ironically, at the very same time Duwelz was putting *SS-Standartenführer* insignia on Degrelle's uniform,[13] he received a message from Charles Generet[14] that Himmler, almost unrecognisable in civvies, was getting ready to leave after his short stay there.

Given the situation, Degrelle reached out to Dr Rudolf Brandt[15] and passed him a memorandum originally written for the chief of the *SS*.

The document included suggestions expressed earlier:

---

11   The acronym for Heinrich Himmler's rank – *SS-Reichsführer*.

12   de Bruyne, op. cit., p. 252.

13   Degrelle was promoted to *SS-Standartenführer* on 20 April 1945.

14   A doctor of philology and classical literature – and a Latin and Greek professor – he fought in the ranks of the *Wallonien* Assault Brigade as *SS-Untersturmführer*. An instructor at the Kienschlag-Neweklau Military Academy, he accompanied Degrelle during his flight to Denmark at the beginning of May 1945. Immediately after the war, he enlisted into the French Foreign Legion. He fought in its ranks and he died in Indochina in 1948.

15   *SS-Standartenführer* – a personal advisor to Heinrich Himmler and the department chief in the Reich's Ministry of Interior.

- stopping the Russians from taking the Walloon and Flemish Legionnaires prisoner and, consequently, a recall of the entire formation north to the Hamburg – Lubeck line and its reform
- allowing the Walloons to settle in Germany after the war so that they could avoid Soviet repressions
- issuing each Legionnaire a payment of 1,000 to 2,000 Reichsmarks to help them survive in this difficult time
- allowing Degrelle himself to leave for Sweden or Portugal by way of air or sea (for securities) and giving him a second last name – Tcherkassy, which he'd be able to use living abroad after the war
- as far as possible, helping the families of those who had found themselves with no means to live after the war[16]

Wanting to take care of as many of his men as possible, Degrelle renewed his efforts to supervise the *SS-Kampfgruppe 'Langemarck'*. On 30 April 1945, he was asked to defend its interests before Brandt. For that reason the Flemish were mentioned in the memorandum as well. Degrelle had done so to gain their acceptance of his command. Brandt's answer was to order the remnants of the two divisions, *'Langemarck'* and *'Wallonien'*, to merge under their respective COs around Bad-Segeberg.

That last condition brought a firm protest from Degrelle, who had been expecting to take command and responsibility for the whole formation. Hahn was hard-pressed to convince him that even if his political efforts were justified, the entire undertaking had ceased to be possible from a military point of view. If you believe Generet, a witness of these events, Degrelle did not receive permission, as he had wanted, to use the new surname with the 'von' preposition. Degrelle felt so strongly about this, he even mentioned the subject during his meetings in Copenhagen with the Chief of Danish Police, Gunther Pancke.

Meanwhile, in the besieged Berlin, *Fuhrer* of the Third Reich Adolf Hitler took his own life. The Walloon leader learned of this in Bad-Segeberg. The field radio station also carried the message that Himmler had been removed from power. This fact was very surprising to Dr Rudolf Brandt who then tried to keep it a secret. In broad terms, Degrelle and his men became a rather awkward problem to the *SS-Reichsführer* and his people on the eve of their inevitable defeat.

The first meeting with Himmler, in Malente on 2 May 1945, brought no

---

16   de Bruyne, op. cit., p. 254.

84.   Dr Werner Best (second on the left) – the Third Reich's agent for Denmark.

progress. Then came an unexpected series of changes. It was decided they would return to Bad-Segeberg to spend the night and then go to Lubeck the next day. The result was yet another trip to Malente. This time Degrelle was a little more fortunate... by complete coincidence he bumped into Himmler's motorcade and was received with open affection. As Hitler was dead already, Leon Degrelle assured Himmler that he and his men were still loyal. These assurances, however, were obviously just the prelude to further claims Degrelle had been addressing to all authorities he could. Himmler promised Degrelle he would do everything within his power to make Degrelle's and his division's return to Denmark possible.[17]

However, as we've said before, it was impossible to talk about the journey of the entire *'Wallonien'* Division, or what was left of it anyway, since Degrelle had only two men with him.

---

17   Ibid., p. 256.

85.   A post-war photograph of Leon Degrelle in an *SS-Standartenführer's* uniform. (Jacques Grancher publishing house archives)

Dr Werner Best,[18] the Reich's agent for Denmark, was tasked with supervising Degrelle's evacuation to Copenhagen. On the night of 2 May, Degrelle was to follow the *SS-Reichsführer's* motorcade on the way from Malente to Flensburg. After their arrival in Kiel, the motorcade had to stop since the RAF had bombarded that large port city. In the darkness, Degrelle's small all-terrain Volkswagen had lost contact with Himmler's entourage and his powerful limousines. As if that wasn't enough, Degrelle's car broke. Degrelle and Generet went to find help, while Duwelz and the Walloon driver remained behind to watch their luggage. In Flensburg, Degrelle acquired a new car with a German driver. This allowed Degrelle to relieve the Walloon chauffeur who had been driving him and his men so far.

On the afternoon of 3 May 1945, the documents were finally ready. Crossing the border was going to be more difficult, however. Degrelle was growing impatient – and he let it show. He managed to convince a colonel responsible

---

18 Werner Best was captured by the Allies after the war and turned over to the Danish authorities. In 1948 he was sentenced to death for his crimes on the Danish people. The sentence was not carried out, however. In 1951, under pressure from West Germany, Best was released and he moved to Mulhein an der Ruhr, where he worked as a procurer for the Hugo Stinnes company. In 1958, the West German de-Nazification Court ordered Best to pay a fine of 70,000 marks for his membership in the *SS* command. In 1969, Best was arrested and charged for organising mass murders in occupied Poland. In 1972, however, he was released again for medical reasons, though the charges were never formally withdrawn.

for all transport to Denmark to join him – and the colonel's presence made their trip to Copenhagen somewhat easier. They went together all the way to Nyborg, where Degrelle had to take the ferry. There was a cargo ship transporting Danish political prisoners, escorted by the Swedish Red Cross, but Degrelle chose not to board it, quite reasonably, too. With some difficulty, he found and boarded a ship transporting *Wehrmacht* troops. On 4 May 1945 at 1:00 a.m. he finally arrived in Copenhagen. He rested a little in the embassy and met with Dr Best at 1:00 p.m. He wanted him to hear his plan, which he had been working on for the last couple of days, one last time and get his approval. Degrelle was very happy with the result, which was an offer to go to Norway. He could even take a team of Walloon war reporters, under the command of the Legion's officer, Franz Chome, who had mysteriously turned up in the Danish capital.

When he was done dealing with the German intendant in Denmark, Degrelle met a new obstacle in the shape of Panacke, who was asking difficult questions about Degrelle's family and future. Degrelle proved himself to be a man who cares deeply for his friends; the safety of his men was just as important to him as his own. He used all his contacts with political or military dignitaries of various levels to seek support for his goals.

It would seem so, however, that Degrelle was unaware that his great dilemma had lost its importance. He was still being received with kindness, but nothing more.

In the evening, Generet was sent on a mission to Copenhagen. He and his driver had then disappeared in the crowds on the streets of the capital.

And so Leon Degrelle had only one companion left: Sergeant Robert Duwelz, who had been his faithful bearer since Degrelle personally promised him a promotion to Captain. Both men reached Oslo, where on the night of 7 May they boarded a plane to Spain. In the meantime, Henri Derriks, taken prisoner by the Allies, was probing the Americans about the possibility of joining their fight against Japan.[19]

On 3 May at 10:30 a.m. the 400 veterans from *Kampfgruppe 'Wallonien'*, many of them wounded, arrived at Schwerin. Almost immediately they surrendered and became POWs.[20] The rest of them scattered on the roads near Schwerin and Lubeck. Many of them had taken civilian clothing, disposing of their uniforms and military documents. Even earlier they had equipped themselves with papers confirming their status as forced workers.

---

19 de Bruyne, op. cit., p. 259.
20 de Bruyne, Eddy, Rikmenspoel, Mark, *For Rex and Belgium* ... (Solihull, 2004), p. 303.

SS-Standartenführer Leon Degrelle had lived the remainder of his life in Spain until the day he died on 31 March 1994.[21]

---

21 In November 1944, the Belgian Court sentenced Degrelle *in absentia* to the death penalty for his collaboration with German occupants. After the war Degrelle tried to get a retrial, but the Belgian authorities denied him. In emigration, Degrelle was considered to be an active neo-Nazi. He wrote a few books and he pursued revisionist and nationalistic journalism (negating or diminishing the crime of the Holocaust). (ed.)

Appendix I

Casualties

We'd be amiss if we didn't give a few lines to the casualties the 28th *SS*-Grenadier Division *'Wallonien'* had suffered during their fight in the Western Pomerania. The list is represented in the following table:[1]

Time	Theatre of operations	Battle strength	KIA	WIA	Sick or unable to fight	Casualties in percentage
05/02-07/03/1945	Stargard area	1800	120	150	200	26
16-20/03/1945	Altdamm bridgehead	650	22	84	-	16
20-14/04/1945	Counter-attack near Schillersdorf	550	98	160	-	47
27/04/45	Counter-attack near Schönwerder	350	10	50	-	17

The statistics presented above perfectly encapsulate the fact that the aforementioned period of several days of battle in the areas of Moczyły [Schillersdorf] / Rosówek [Neu-Rosow] / Kamieniec [Schöningen] were very bloody and fierce. *Kampfgruppe 'Derriks'* had lost nearly half of its already thinning complement.

---

1   Mabire, Jean, *Division de Choc Wallonie, Lutte á Mort en Poméranie* (ed. Jacques Grancher, 1996), p. 362.

Appendix II

Charles Verpoorten – in Search of my Father[1]

M y father, Albert Verpoorten, was a member of the Rexist Party and a pilot in the Belgian Army. When the war had started he decided to remain in the country. Since he was also a journalist, he worked with the majority of the Belgian media that collaborated with the Nazis.

In August of 1943, he joined the contingent of Walloon volunteers, who left for the Eastern Front to fight the Soviet Union. He remained there until 1943, serving as a war correspondent. Afterwards, he had been demobilised by Leon Degrelle and took on the duties of the chief of staff for the *Juenesses Legionnaires*.[2] At the end of 1944, Degrelle had sent my father to the *SS-Junkerschule* in Sofienwalde, where he was promoted to the rank of *SS-Untersturmführer*. March of 1945 my father spent in Berlin and he accompanied Degrelle several times, when the latter was visiting Division *'Wallonien's'* troops on the front.[3]

On 22 April 1945, *SS-Sturmbannführer* Henri Derriks, the commanding officer of *Kampfgruppe 'Derriks'*, asked *'Wallonien'* Division's command for 20 soldiers to cover the retreat of the Walloon and Flemish troops near Rosówek. Given that all these officers were my father's friends from the Christus Rex Party and that they all had volunteered together, he chose to join them as well. That same afternoon, the group took positions around Rosówek. During the Russian shelling, my father jumped into a foxhole with three other soldiers to take cover from shrapnel. One of these soldiers was my father's close friend, *SS-Obersturmführer* GePe. At some point a shell exploded in their hole. Two of the four soldiers died instantly and GePe received fatal wounds. He could hear my father's whisper: 'My arms'. Then, GePe had left the foxhole and, ignoring his many injuries, helped by a Flemish volunteer, he covered the 1,500 metres that separated him from Derriks's command post. Once there, he asked Derriks to

---

1   The text was written by Charles Verpoorten who had passed it to the author for publishing in their correspondence from 14 November 2012.
2   A youth organisation of the Christus Rex party.
3   According to Eddy de Bruyne, in March and April of 1945, Leon Degrelle was seldom seen on the front. When he was there, it was mainly for propaganda reasons.

86.   Albert Verpoorten in a *Jeunesses Legionnaires* uniform, 1941. (Charles Verpoorten's collection)

send somebody for my father. Afterwards, he had lost consciousness and was evacuated to a field hospital in Prenzlau. GePe survived the war and lived in Belgium, where he died on 3 May 2011.

According to Derriks's memoires, he had sent a medic to get my father but the medic was killed on his way. When Derriks himself had arrived at the place, he found my father dead. A soldier named Bayard took his documents.

After the war, my mother (I have four siblings, my youngest sister was born in February of 1945 in Hanover) wanted to know more about the fate of her husband. She asked her brother-in-law, a priest, to investigate the matter. By the end of 1945, my uncle had visited several Belgian prisons to speak with the members of the Walloon Legion.

Having talked with Derriks and GePe, he confirmed that my father must have died on that day. In order to receive an official statement from the court to formalise my father's death and acknowledge my mother as a widow, he asked Henri Derriks to write the appropriate testimony. In 1947, my father was officially proclaimed dead. This did not stop the vetting investigators, however,

le 10 octobre 1946

Déclaration

Je soussigné, DERRIKS,Henry-Marie-Joseph né à Roclenge sur Geer, le 31 juillet 1904, et y domicilié rue Jean Derriks, certifie les faits suivants :

Le 23 avril 1945, alors que j'étais commandeur du premier Bataillon du 69ème Régiment de la Légion Wallonie, avoir participé, avec une partie de mon unité au combat du hameau de NEU-ROSSOW, situé à 30Kms environ au S.E. de STETTIN(Poméranie), combat au cours duquel le lieutenant Albert VERPOORTEN(originaire de Huy) et à ce moment, membre de la Légion Wallonie, fut tué dans les circonstances suivantes :

"Dans le courant de l'après-midi, vers 14h30, je fus prévenu que le lieutenant G   P   venait d'être gravement blessé et je m'occupais aussitôt de l'évacuation de cet officier, qui fut enlevé dans la ligne de feu par mes brancardiers et évacué vers l'arrière dans une de nos autos-blindées. Sitôt après l'évacuation de P   je quittai mon P.C. pour inspecter mes positions, battues en ce moment avec violence par les canons des chars russes de l'artillerie russe. Je causai un moment en passant auprès du lieutenant VERPOORTEN et continuai à suivre le front de ma position . A mon retour, alors que j'allai atteindre l'endroit où VERPOORTEN se trouvait, un obus éclata entre nous. Je fus jeté à terre et quand je me relevai, je m'adressai à VERPOORTEN auquel je vis une blessure à la tête, région frontale. Je lui dis d'attendre et filai à mon P.C. chercher du secours; j'envoyai un bran-cardier chercher le lieutenant, mais mon émissaire fut tué en cours de route. Ne le voyant pas revenir, je me rendis une nouvelle fois auprès de VERPOORTEN et je dus constater que celui-ci venait de mourir. L'attaque russe s'intensifiant je dus me rendre à d'autres endroits pour y remplir mon commandement. Je ne me rendis plus par la suite à l'endroit VERPOORTEN où VERPOORTEN fut tué .

J'ai appris par après qu'un nommé BAYARD sergent à la légion s'était assuré des papiers du lieutenant, mais BAYARD fut également blessé et évacué. Je ne l'ai plus revu dans la suite .

Le corps du lieutenant VERPOORTEN est resté sur le terrain et a été vraisemblablement inhumé par la population de NEU-ROSSOW .

Henry DERRIKc
Major à la Légion Wallonie

87.   Henri Derriks's statement on Albert Verpoorten's fate.
(Charles Verpoorten's collection)

from keeping up my father's death sentence for collaboration up until 1964.

When I was 17, my mother had told me of my father's fate, about his service in *'Wallonien'* Division and about his death in Poland. I decided I wanted to know more and so I met with many former soldiers of that formation, including GePe, Derriks and even Leon Degrelle. Only the two former had confirmed my father's death, even though their recollections were not all that consistent. Whatever the case, I was certain my dad was dead and I was now only interested in visiting the site of his death and maybe even finding his remains around Rosówek. For the longest time, unfortunately, I did not have the chance to make the trip as long as Poland and West Germany remained behind the Iron Curtain.

Several years after my mother had passed away, I decided to continue my search. I was a journalist almost all my life and I plan to produce a documentary of these last days of battle over the Oder.

After profound analysis of Division *'Wallonien's'* history and with the help of such historians as Eddy de Bruyne or Robert Balsam, I planned my trip to

88.   Charles Verpoorten with his sisters in the military cemetery
at Glinna. (Charles Verpoorten's collection)

Poland. During the first trip I managed to locate the site of my father's 'death'. I also visited many of the cemeteries in the area (from what Derriks had told me, my father might have been buried by some of the locals). I found the grave sites of many of the Flemish soldiers from the 27th *SS*-Volunteer Division *'Langemarck'* and that was all. In the town of Glinna, where there is a German War Cemetery, I found a list of names of the soldiers buried there. I found my father's name among them.

In Glinna, I was put in contact with Piotr Brzeziński, a member of the Pomerania 1945 Association, a group of military archaeologists who handle exhumations of nameless grave sites. After a couple of months I returned to Poland with a film crew and met with Piotr in Szczecin. I managed to receive permission to study the area of the fighting near Rosówek, Moczyły and Kamieniec. Luckily, the terrain had not changed much since the war. We had to postpone the entire operation, though, because a part of the field was under cultivation and the owner did not allow us to work because of the harvest. I decided to continue my investigation of the Belgian archives. I had delivered my application and after a few months wait I received permission from the Belgian Ministry of Justice to view my father's file.

89.   A collection of personal items belonging to Albert Verpoorten
(currently in his son's possession). (Charles Verpoorten's collection)

There were a couple of objects, apparently found with his body: a rosary, a pencil, a mirror, a comb, some pictures of my mother, etc. Among them I also found a document suggesting there should be also my father's *SS* dog-tags, number 8,020, which was still missing, however. I finally concluded that *SS-Scharfuhrer* Bayard must have taken it (he was there with my father), which was a definite proof that my father was indeed killed where I thought he was. All these materials, however, were not convincing enough for the vetting investigators, who were still doubtful of my father being dead.

In the file, I also found an envelope dated 1947, containing a handful of documents from the archives in Berlin, tasked by the Belgian Ministry of Reconstruction to search for the Belgians who went missing in Germany and Poland. One of these documents was a Rex Party membership card and a couple of orders from the beginning of April 1945.

I went through the archives of the Ministry of Reconstruction, where I found additional information on my father: copies of some documents from the Ministry of Justice and a handful of medical documents which were never released to the Vetting Court.

These documents (tags placed on the bodies of wounded soldiers) became

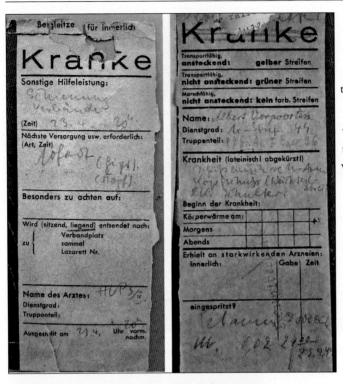

90.   ID tags were placed by medics on wounded soldiers. The tags on the left belonged to Albert Verpoorten – denying his death on the battlefield. (Charles Verpoorten's collection)

91.   A document confirming Verpoorten's admission to the field hospital in Neubrandenburg. (Charles Verpoorten's collection)

proof that my father did not die, in fact, on 23 March 1945, but had been found alive by the medics around 8:00 p.m. (having been wounded probably around 2:00 p.m.) and evacuated to the medical post around midnight. Tags, both from the medical post as well as the field hospital in Neubrandenburg, where my father had been transported to in the next 24 hours, list his injuries.

In the meantime, I managed to go to Rosówek. During our excavations we found the remains of several soldiers from *'Langemarck'* Division.

As for my father's fate, together with Eddy de Bruyne and Piotr Brzeziński we had combed through the aforementioned evidence. We came up with the following hypotheses:

- on 23 April 1945, my father was evacuated from the medical post (*Hauptverbrandplatz, HVP 3/II*) to Neubrandenburg. Unfortunately, we were never able to locate the site of the medical post;
- he could have died at the field hospital but there was no documentation that would confirm that;
- he was killed, when the field hospital was bombed
- he was taken prisoner by the Russians on 27 April 1945, when the Soviets

92.   Charles Verpoorten during field research in Rosówek
[Neu-Rosow]. (Charles Verpoorten's collection)

93.   Another photograph taken during excavations in Rosówek [Neu-Rosow]. (Charles Verpoorten's collection)

took the town. He was then transported to Russia, where he died in a POW camp.

Even now, I am still trying to find new evidence and clues in the various archives, hoping to find my father's burial site. At the end of June 2012, VBGO[4] exhumed remains of 35 soldiers from the cemetery of the old hospital in Neubrandenburg, several of which are yet to be identified. In order to see if my father's body was among them, we still await the results of DNA tests.

---

4   *Verein für Bergung Gefallener in Osteuropa* – a German association of military archaeologists.

Appendix III

Andre Regibeau – I Wish to Speak with You, Friends[1]

I would like to talk about the third generation of idealists, who took the place of their predecessors. These young men enlisted into our ranks and joined the legion in Wołowo [Wolhau] in October of 1944. They were first entrusted to Jacques Capelle who was able to take advantage of their good will and their desire to learn. He managed to train them so well that after only a few weeks they formed a company deserving note. Their enthusiasm, attitude and their desire to prove themselves worthy of their ancestors were admirable. Indeed, almost all of them had taken part in numerous youth camps in the past, which is where their strong sense of solidarity and friendship was stemming from.

Unfortunately, due to the legion's reorganisation, Jacques Capelle passed his command to me. The company was almost entirely comprised of his trainees. Afterwards, Capelle became the commanding officer of the 7th Company, which several months later, in February of 1945, was heroically fending off attacks of Russian tanks near the Lindenberg hill in the Western Pomerania.

These young 'rookies of history' did not lack for courage and boldness. They took great pleasure in showing off before German peasants, who admired them, listening to their marching songs in the style of *Pompons-merde ...*

The audience was moved by the young men's actions and clapped. They thought the marching song was *schon, sehr schon*!

At the end of January 1945, they marched to the Eastern Front. From February all the way to the end of the war, the company engaged in many fierce, ever more desperate, battles. I wish to express my overwhelming admiration for all these young men, survivors and the fallen alike. They all fought to the extent of their abilities.

I would prefer to name them all. As it is not possible, however, I shall mention only a few ... J. Agnessens was badly wounded when he joined our lines

---

1   Regibeau, Andre, *Je Veux Parler de Vous, Amis ...* [in:] *'Le temeraire'*, issue 30, November/December 1985. Given the historical value of this material and because so far it has been known to so few readers, we publish it here in its entirety.

94.   A very rare photograph showing Andre Regibeau in the rank of *SS-Unterscharführer*. One should pay note to the early version of the '*Totenkopf*' skull on his forage cap and the '*Edelweiss*' on the left shoulder of his uniform jacket. (Michel le Roy's collection)

in Dąbie, never laying down his weapons. I can still hear him as he speaks to me in the basement, where he was being treated: 'You will tell my friends I had thought of them before I died, won't you, sir. I so want to live for them and for our organisation'. I can also remember his comrade, Nechelput, who was killed, too. And that little Warnimont. Then Descurieux and Hannebique, who remained behind at the Soviet lines and were presumed dead. They came back two days later, however, with an enemy patrol on their tail. And I remember my communications officers, Thuilliez and Leplae, always at the ready, always in good spirits, their eyes never wet. I was wounded on 20 April 1945 and Thuilliez came to my rescue. He was injured, too – caught a bullet which was most definitely aimed at me. He said to me 'We'll go back to the hospital together'. He survived but had to go back to France. Did he really die in Indochina?

I will always see right next to me, over there in Strzyżno, Froment and Anthonissen. He is leaning on his machine gun and returning hellish fire. So many names ... Larose brothers, G. Aussems, P. Moreau, whom I believed to be

95.   A Walloon *SS-Mann* of Polish origins – Johan Stawinski. (Michel le Roy's collection)

gone and who luckily managed to come through the net.[2] Busiau imprisoned in Strzebielewo, R. Bustin, A. Braibant, G. Wouters, Chr. Havet, Delhez, Deridder, de Surlemont brothers imprisoned in Żarowo. Bukowski – the Pole,[3] Claude Leroy,[4] who died in Dąbie on 18 March 1945.

It was Claude Leroy's death that hit me the hardest throughout the whole war. The moment little Descurieux told me what had happened, I retrieved Leroy's body and we buried him, while still under bombardment, near the command post. Today, he may be the one person deserving a monument?

I have to mention Rommel and Montgomery [sic], too, the former soldiers of Estonia. The dare-devils. They were a little older. One of them was a stubborn bastard. Both of them had foul mouths. They were boasting their famous names (fake, no doubt). But we do owe Rommel a lot. It was him that so perfectly covered our last group's retreat from Żarowo in March 1945.

---

2   Regibeau means Soviet patrols.
3   We know of at least two names of Polish volunteers, who served in the Division *'Wallonien'*: Bernard Witkowski, born 21 March 1920 in Poznań, and Johan Stawinski, born in 1921 in the Belgian city of Liége.
4   Younger brother of Jacques Leroy.

I also cannot forget about a group of several dozen Frenchmen, who had joined our ranks in Oberhausen, mid-January 1945. Discouraged by their training in Wildflecken[5] and enamoured by the Walloon Legion's reputation, they were determined to stay with us. I did all I could to integrate them with our people. I put a Walloon Sergeant, Renard, in charge of them and named a French Corporal Pierre Lemaire as his second. He was wounded but he joined us soon nonetheless. He was a volunteer from Oder 1945. Some of these men had names of legendary knights, like Eudes, Roland. Only three of them survived until the end of the war: Roland, Lemaire and Morineau, a Parisian *titi*,[6] who was so great at telling funny stories. Brousse and Eudes died at Strzyżno on 4 March 1945 on our forward position. Before he died, Ougraud, a former anti-aircraft gunner, had done something incredible: leaning on the shoulder of his friend, he used his machine gun to shoot down a Russian fighter plane as it was making a sharp turn on our flank. The machine crashed a little farther away and we all went over there to see the wreckage. Ougraud is yet another of my mates who had ended his short life in Strzyżno, hit by a Russian shovel. The Soviets kept popping up everywhere and he couldn't escape them.

I also wish to tell the story of four Germans. Surprised on their leave by the advancing Red Army, they joined our ranks spontaneously. I assigned all four to Pierre Hancisse's platoon. They were accepted easily and we became close very soon.

This is confirmed by the following fact: one of the Germans, chosen as our guide since he was raised in these parts, was to lead the assault. It was in the middle of February. Before we marched, he said: 'I'll be back'. He kept his word and after the attack had failed, he returned to our ranks. From the four Germans, three had lost their lived in Strzyżno. They died defending their own land.

Finally, I wish to speak of a couple of Flemish soldiers, who served with our company. In the chaos of the end of the war, some would lose their units and join others. Over Oder, their first time in the East, the Flemish and Walloons fought side by side. It was a symbol. The Flemish were with us over Oder in Kołbaskowo during our assault of Pomelen on 20 April 1945. I can't remember the names of our Flemish friends, who were with us there. One thing, however, will forever be etched into my memory. In the afternoon of 20 April, during our counter-attack, I walked behind a Flemish gunnery corporal a long way. He was fighting right in front of me. A rather portly boy, he had red cheeks. I can still see him, sweating in

---

5   French units of the *33rd SS-Grenadier Division 'Charlemagne'* trained there.
6   An archetype of Gavroche, a Parisian rouge, audacious and bold.

the foxhole, at the far edge of the battlefield, opposite the Oder. That was where he died from a bullet that hit his chest.

Who can tell me his name?

Appendix IV

Spanish Odyssey

The Walloon leader, Leon Degrelle, took interest in recruiting the Spanish in the middle of 1944, when his division required reinforcements due to the casualties they suffered at the Eastern Front. He tasked two of the division's officers with the recruitment: Alphonse van Horembeke and Paul Kehren, both of whom fought for the Frankists in the Civil War.[1] In September, they travelled all over Germany, finally finding a group of Spaniards from the old 'Ghost Battalion'[2] in Stockerau, near Vienna. At the end of 1944, in a Berlin hotel, Leon Degrelle met with two Spanish officers: Luis Garcia Valdajos and Richardo Botet (who was a translator and knew German and French very well). Valdajos, immediately accepted by Degrelle into his formation as *SS-Obersturmführer*, was tasked with the recruitment of his countrymen. On 1 November 1944, the Spaniards left for Breslau, where the *'Wallonien'* Division's training camp was. The next week the entire unit was transported west to the Alfed-Leine area, near Hanover.

Meanwhile, Spanish volunteers recruited by Garcia Valdajos and his co-workers started to flock to the formation as it was being built. Valdajos gave them basic instruction and organised them into the 'Spanish Company'. Richardo Botet Moro and two former Blue Division officers, Lorenzo Ocania and Rafel Lafuente became platoon leaders. The three received the ranks of senior enlisted officers, *SS-Oberscharführer*. At the time, the company's complement was around a hundred Spaniards and their numbers grew to some 240 as time went by.[3] In the meantime, Richardo Botet Moro was sent to the *SS-Panzergrenadier* school in Prosetschniz in Czechoslovakia. After graduation he was promoted to the rank of *Standarten Oberjunker*.[4]

In the middle of November, the Spanish recruits were sent to a training camp

---

1   <http://www.historycy.org/historia/index.php/t47951.html> [date of access: 08/06/2013].
2   The 'Ghost Battalion' ('Bataillon Fantasma') was created in the middle of 1944. Formed in Hall in Tirol, near Innsbruck, the battalion's fate is not well known. We do know that one company of the battalion fought against Tito's Partisans in Yugoslavia, and another one in Romania and Czechoslovakia. The company was obliterated in the fighting.
3   Norling, Erik, *The Story of a Spanish Waffen-SS Officer ...* [in:] *Siegrunen Magazine*, issue 79.
4   Martinez, Gil Eduardo M., *The Spanish in the SS and Wehrmacht 19440 1945*, p. 78.

96. *SS-Standarten Oberjunker* Richardo Botet Moro. (Author's own collection)

in Hemmendorf/Olendorf, while Garcia Valdajos returned to Berlin to take care of some administrative issues. On 25 December 1944, a year after the start of the German offensive in the Ardennes, the Spaniards were deployed with the Walloons to Belgium. Because of the Germans' failures the offensive was aborted at the beginning of January. The Spanish and the Walloons returned to their previous stations.

At the end of January 1945, in light of the quick advance of the Soviet offensive, the *Kampfgruppe 'Wallonien'*, consisting of two *SS* grenadier regiments (69th and 70th) and the 28th *SS*-Artillery Regiment, was deployed to Pomerania to address the threat at the front-line. The Spaniards were assigned to the 3rd Company in the 1st Battalion of the 70th *SS*-Grenadier Regiment, under the command of *SS-Obersturmführer* Robert Deny.

SS-Oberscharfuhrers La Fuente and Lorenzo Ocanas and *Standarten Oberjunker* Richardo Botet Moro became the leaders of the three platoons operating in the first line. The fourth platoon was assigned as back-up for the 1st Company in the 1st Battalion of the 70th *SS*-Grenadier Regiment. Its leader was *SS-Hauptscharfuhrer* Abel Ardoos. The Spanish *SS* were very well equipped and ready for battle. They were armed with machine guns, *panzerfausts* and ... a field

97.   A post-war photograph of Miguel Ezquerra Sanchez – *Kampfgruppe 'Ezquerra's'* Commanding Officer during battle in a besieged Berlin. (Author's own collection)

kitchen.[5]

Garcia Valdajos was still in Berlin at the time, acquiring documents in order to marry his German fiancée. Aside from that he was also busy with various administrative activities, since his organisational talents were much greater than his combat prowess.[6] Which is why, in his absence, the command of the Spanish company was given to *SS-Untersturmführer* Rudi Bal, a Spanish-speaking Belgian officer born in Argentina. Bal was killed in action on 6 March 1945 and was supposedly replaced by another Walloon officer, *SS-Untersturmführer* Albert Steiver, who was the company's CO during the fighting in the Stargard area.[7]

Valdajos rejoined his men during the bloody battles around Kurcewo in February 1945. The Spaniards suffered heavy losses. Only about 60 of them managed to avoid death or capture. When the *'Wallonien'* Division was regrouping in the middle of March 1945, the remaining Spanish volunteers left the formation and returned to their garrison in Alfed-Leine. Later, they regrouped around Potsdam and finally reached Berlin.

While in Berlin, the command of the small group (there were only a 100-

---

5   Ibid., p. 82.
6   Ibid., p. 81.
7   Norling, op. cit.

150 of them) passed to a Spanish *SS* officer – Miguel Ezquerra Sanchez. Garcia Valdajos had been already assigned as liaison officer for the Spanish volunteers in the *SS* Headquarters. When the Russians came close to the German borders and the encirclement was slowly becoming a fact, *SS-Obersturmführer* Valdajos joined his comrades from *Kampfgruppe 'Ezquerra'*. At the time, *the Kampfgruppe* was fighting near the Reich Chancellery alongside the remnants of the 15th Latvian Fusilier Battalion of the *Waffen-SS*. Many of the Spanish volunteers were killed or taken prisoner by the Soviets during the fighting. Valdajos reached the Spanish Embassy, where he hid until 9 May. It wasn't the best hiding place, however, since the Russians were very close and they kept sending Spanish communists serving in the Red Army to take the embassy. And so Valdajos had to run, like many of the *SS*, in civilian clothing, pretending to be a forced worker. Afterwards, he went into hiding until 8 June and then went back to Spain through the Netherlands, Belgium and France. He was sentenced to two years in prison, which he never served. A military court, sympathetic to him, had acquitted him on 1 March 1947.[8]

---

8 Ibid.

Appendix V

Uniforms and Insignia

The Walloons carried the standard patches with the Sign runes on their mess jackets, reserved for the *Waffen-SS*. It is worthy of note, though, that in August or September of 1944, the new recruits from the reserve battalion, while they were forming their division, received a small batch of patches with the Burgundian Cross. These insignia were never officially approved though and never came into common use among the front-line troops.[1]

There were also insignia that distinguished the Walloons among other German or foreign formations gathered under the *Waffen-SS* banner. On their sleeves they wore a shield in Belgians colours (black, yellow and red) and an armband with the name of the unit, if only on paper.

The shield came in two patterns. The earlier one, already in use when the Legion was functioning as part of the *Wehrmacht*, was mechanically woven using the BEVO[2] technique. Because the material was so thin, it was usually first glued or sewn onto a cloth underlay and then onto the uniform. The second pattern was simplified – being mechanically embroidered on a much thicker material and placed on the uniform directly. In literature, it is accepted that the first pattern belonged to *the* Walloon Legion, while the other one belonged to the Brigade and *SS*-Division *'Wallonien'*.[3] Both versions, however, were in use in the *SS*. By regulation, the shield was placed on the left arm, right under the eagle, or the 'V' patch, for the ranks of *SS-Sturmann* and *Rottenfuhrer*. Sometimes the soldiers would wear it on their forearms, but that was an exception rather than rule.[4] It should be mentioned that the available iconographic material from the Burgundians' fight in Western Pomerania does not show any soldiers wearing these insignia. Therefore the use of them in that particular theatre of war should be treated as nothing more than hypothesis.

A commonly seen detail of the *Waffen-SS* uniform was an armband with the name of the unit, worn on the left cuff of the uniform jacket or coat, but the

---

1   Eddy de Bruyne's letter to the author from 15 November 2012.
2   This method's name comes from the acronym of the name of a factory in Wuppertal, where the Third Reich's uniform insignia were manufactured – Bandfabrik Ewald Vorsteher.
3   Williamson, Gordon, *The Waffen-SS, 24 to 38 Divisions & Volunteer Legions*, p. 13.
4   Eddy de Bruyne's letter to the author from 12 November 2012.

99.   An original Walloon national shield –
the first pattern. (Michel le Roy's collection)

98.   A page from a '*Soldbuch*' of a Walloon
soldier wearing a Burgundian Cross patch
on his collar. (Eddy de Bruyne's collection)

101.   A modern replica of a '*Wallonien*'
BEVO armband. (Author's own collection)

100.   A Walloon national shield showing
the second pattern. (Osprey Publishing)

latter was rare. The armband was made from a black tape, 28 mm wide and 49 cm long. The armband allowed for easier identification of soldiers from particular formations. It also had a positive influence on the forming of a strong *esprit de corps* among the *Waffen-SS* troops.[5] The commanding officer of a unit would issue these armbands during official ceremonies, reminding the soldier receiving it that he was being awarded an enormous honour. The specific criteria by which units were allowed to have their own armbands are still unknown. It is probable that *SS-Reichsführer* Heinrich Himmler personally evaluated each application and decided whether a unit had the right to wear an armband.[6] The armbands were made using several techniques: manual embroidery with an aluminium wire or thread, mechanically embroidered with white or silvery grey thread, mechanically woven with aluminium grey cotton or silk thread.[7]

As for the use of these armbands in *'Wallonien'* Division, we only know that Leon Degrelle had a one-of-a-kind armband with the name 'Wallonie', manually embroidered in Gothic script, probably custom-made. Regular armbands were approved for production in 1944.[8] It is also well known that they were produced and issued from warehouses, but the photographic proof for their factual use are scarce.[9] The author knows of only one such picture showing *SS-Untersturmführer* Leon Gillis wearing an armband made in the BEVO technique on his uniform jacket. The original Walloon armbands are a rarity on the collector's market, which goes to show how few of them were produced.

It is interesting that the serial armbands bear the name *'Wallonien'*,[10] while Leon Degrelle's armband (as well as shoulder-shields) say 'Wallonie'.[11]

There is a curiosity worth to be mentioned at this point. The Walloon Legion, fighting in the structures of the *Wehrmacht* as the 373rd Infantry Battalion, was incorporated into the Mountain Corps[12] operating in the Caucasus in 1942. Because of that the Legionnaires were permitted to wear a patch characteristic for the mountain troops, *Edelweiss*,[13] on their right arm. After the legion's incorporation into the *SS*, the veterans were allowed to keep the patch on their

---

5   Lumsden, Robin, *Waffen-SS – Organizacja, Działania Bojowe, Umundurowanie*, p. 77.
6   Ibid., p. 78.
7   Ibid., p. 79.
8   Ibid., p. 80.
9   Williamson, op. cit., p. 13.
10   German spelling.
11   French spelling.
12   This is probably the XXXXIX (the original Roman notation of the number 49 in the *Wehrmacht*) Mountain Corps, also known as Alpine. (ed.)
13   A flower growing in many European mountains.

102.   A Walloon Legionnaire with the mountain rifleman's '*Edelweiss*' sewn onto his sleeve. [This photograph is missing a credit]

uniforms. This is why the Division '*Wallonien*' can be considered the only formation in the German military to have an actual mountain insignia without actually being mountain troops. Furthermore, the *Edelweiss* pattern for the *Wehrmacht* was different from the *Waffen-SS* pattern, making the Walloons doubly unique.[14]

Another characteristic element in the equipment of the Walloon volunteers from the *Waffen-SS*, which could be seen on several photographs (including those from Western Pomerania) is a fur jacket made from sheepskin. They were worn by, among others, the company commanders Leon Gillis and Andre Regibeau. As for Gillis, he got his coat from a local boy in Cherkassy. This particular clothing was difficult to acquire and in high demand, especially during winter months. It was a symbol of prestige, proof that the owner had to be *alter Tcherkassy-Kampfer*,[15] since that was the only region the Walloons could find it.

These things were so valuable that their owners would sew a note into the underside of their coats. The note would name the comrade[16] the coat was supposed to pass to if the owner was killed. We may even suppose that these

14   Littlejohn, David, *Foreign Legions of the Third Reich*, vol. 2, p. 120.
15   A veteran of the Cherkassy Cauldron.
16   Eddy de Bruyne's letter to the author from 12 November 2012.

103.　A Walloon *SS-Unterscharführer* with a Blood Order pinned to his uniform jacket. (Eddy de Bruyne's collection)

coats were treated as talismans.

The Walloon uniforms sometimes showed a unique badge – the Walloon Honour Badge (also known as the 'Blood Order'). It was created in 1941. The badge shows the Burgundian cross and a sword placed in a circle, with a French inscription: *Bravoure, Honeur, Fidelite*.[17] It wasn't, in fact, an official military award but a 'political' one given to the members of the paramilitary *Formations de Combat* within the structure of the Rexist Party. The badge was officially approved by *SS-Reichsführer* Heinrich Himmler on 16 October 1944. Nonetheless, it was in use long before that.

The order came in three classes: bronze, silver and gold. The bronze badge was available to the privates of the Walloon Legion, who had served in the *Formations de Combat* before 8 August 1941.[18] The silver badge was awarded to officers by the same rules as the bronze one. The gold badge was for senior officers and politicians who showed they deserved it by some extraordinary deed.[19]

Leon Degrelle and an unnamed Walloon chaplain were the only ones to receive the Gold Blood Order. We also know of one order of the gold class with

17　Courage, Honour, Loyalty.
18　The date of the legion's deployment to the Eastern Front.
19　Eddy de Bruyne's letter to the author from 29 January 2013.

104.   Leon Degrelle. Among the German medals (such as the Iron Cross, First Class; the Gold Wound Badge; the Assault Infantry Medal; the Gold Close-Combat Clasp; and the Knight's Cross of the Iron Cross), he also wears the Walloon Blood Order. (*Axe & Allies* Magazine)

diamonds. It was awarded to Victor Matthys, who became the leader of the Christus Rex movement after Degrelle's departure to the front.[20]

---

20   <http://axis101.bizland.com/FlemishAward3.html> [date of access: 03/05/2013].

Appendix VI

After the War ...

I n order to properly tell the story of the Walloon soldiers and their fates after the war, we first shall take a closer look at the situation in Belgium at the start of the Second World War.

The invasion by the Third Reich had begun on 10 May 1940 and ended on the 28th of the same month with Belgium's capitulation.[1] Belgian soldiers, who fought against the Germans, immediately became POWs and were sent to various prison camps. Many of them managed to avoid internment and simply became civilians, engaging in a multi-level cooperation with the occupants, starting with propaganda efforts and ending with military service.[2]

In September 1944, when Belgium was liberated by the Anglo-American forces, the Belgian Government decided to punish the citizens who collaborated with the Germans one way or the other. In order to make that happen, the Belgian Security Services, *Surete*, together with the revitalised army, started to hunt all suspected collaborators. The sentences of those arrested during the war, in the years 1944–45 after Belgium's liberation, were not enforced until the end of the conflict. Most of those who were abroad, still fighting on the front, were sentenced *in absentia*. Until they could be taken into the custody of the law enforcement, they were treated and hunted as deserters. After their capture, the majority of them was deported back to Belgium and then sent to prison, once their identities were confirmed. *Surete* was looking for collaborators in Germany as well. For example, Jean Vermeire who, after several months in hiding, was captured and arrested.

In the first weeks after the Third Reich's capitulation, many Walloons, who fought on the side of the Germans, were arrested and sentenced to die. The

---

1 The Belgian King, Leopold III, decided to remain in the occupied country but the government had first evacuated to Paris, then to London. Belgian armed forces under the command of Hubert Pierlot, the Prime Minister in exile, comprised of colonial forces in the Congo and of the 1st Riflemen Battalion formed in Wales, which evolved into the 1st Belgian Brigade in 1943. The brigade took part in combat against the Germans in 1944–45 in France, Belgium, the Netherlands and Northern Germany. (ed.)

2 The Belgian Emigratory Government considered the King, placed under home arrest by the Germans, as unable to rule. In the autumn of 1940, the King met with Hitler but refused to collaborate. After the liberation, he spent the years 1944–50 in emigration. After the controversies which erupted when he had returned to the country, he abdicated. (ed.)

situation had changed a little by the end of 1945 when death sentences were being slowly reduced to long-term imprisonment, as it was happening in other countries as well. The convicted collaborators started to leave their prisons, however, after serving only a couple of years. An example of that was Henri Derriks, who was released from prison and spent the rest of his life living in peace in Belgium. He died on 6 November 1972.[3] As for other heroes of this book, we should mention a few more. Roland Devresse died on 23 October 2001 in Cevennes in the South of France. Andre Regibeau died on 15 February 1987 in a car accident, while on his way to a meeting of the veterans from his unit, which was to take place on 29 November 1986. Frans Hellebaut was already 86 years old when he died on 18 June 1984. His former friends, probably at the family's request,[4] attended the funeral. GePe died on 3 May 2011. Leon Gillis, due to some complications connected to his asthma, met his untimely end on 24 March 1977. He was 64 years old.[5] Jacques Leroy was taken prisoner by the British after the war and he was soon deported to Belgium. After serving his sentence and having been stripped of his basic rights, Leroy left to Germany, where he took German citizenship and moved to Bavaria. He died on 5 August 1996.[6]

The veterans of the 28th *SS-Panzergrenadier* Division *'Wallonien'* tried to defend themselves in local courts arguing that they only fought the Soviet Union and not the Western Allies and certainly not against their own country.[7] It did not do them much good. Belgian law had changed before the end of the war and it was inflexible. The following paragraph was added to one of the codices: 'All who take up arms against the Kingdom of Belgium and her allies are subject to punishment'. The Soviet Union, as an ally of the West, was also automatically an ally of Belgium.[8] After the war, all around the country (including Flanders and Wallonia) some 240 collaborators had been sentenced to die and more than 5,000 were arrested and charged with collaborating with the national socialist regime.[9]

---

3   Michel le Roy's letter to the author from 30 August 2013.
4   Ibid.
5   *Axe & Allies Magazine*, issue 10, 2006, p. 44.
6   Landwehr, Richard, *Siegrunen Magazine*, issue 80, p. 83.
7   The Walloon troops were used on the territories of other Allied countries, in anti-Partisan operations (Poland) and there were plans to employ them as occupying and pacification forces in Belgium should it be retaken by the Germans in the Ardennes offensive in 1944 and 1950. Some of the Walloon units were even transported back to the Western Front at the end of 1944 and nothing suggests they had anything to say in the matter of being used in their own land against Allied forces of the Belgian resistance. (ed.)
8   Charles Verpoorten's letter to the author from 12 March 2013.
9   <http://wyborcza.pl/2029020,76842,11470628.html> [date of access: 12/04/2013].

105.   Jacques Leroy (on the right) in one of the post-war meetings of the '*Wallonien*' Division's veterans. (*39-45* Magazine)

Jacques Leroy's story may serve as a form of summary for the Walloons' fate and the mark their volunteer service in the *Waffen-SS* had left.

The pain from his war wounds hunted Leroy for the rest of his life. When a doctor visited him in his home in 1992, it quickly became clear that the physician was more interested in making 'political speeches' than in helping his patient. The doctor immediately accused Leroy of fighting against his own country. Leroy replied: 'Not in this case. I only fought Bolshevism'. The doctor then said, 'I hope that you're as anti-Nazi now as you were anti-communist then'. Leroy was too surprised to tell him that he only needed medical attention, not a political discussion. In all his statements after the war, Leroy remained loyal to his comrades and never denied his choices or the duty he took on.

Bibliography

Bishop, Chris, *Zagraniczne Formacje SS. Zagraniczni Ochotnicy w Waffen SS w latach 1940-45* (Warsaw: Muza SA, 2008).

Brzeziński, Piotr, *Ocena Szans Operacji Zaczepnej o Kryptonimie 'Sonnenwende' na Podstawie Analizy Możliwości Niemieckich Wojsk Pancernych w Końcowym Etapie II Wojny Światowej. Luty 1945* (<www.pomorze1945.com>) [date of access: 28/03/2013].

De Bruyne, Eddy, Rikmenspoel, Mark, *For Rex and Belgium – Léon Degrelle and Waloon Political & Military Collaboration* (Solihull: Helion & Company Limited, 2004).

De Bruyne, Eddy, *Léon Degrelle et la Légion Wallonie : La fin d'une legend* (Liége: Editions Luc Pire, 2011).

Degrelle, Léon, *Front Wschodni 1941–1945* (Międzyzdroje: Arkadiusz Wingret, 2002).

Degrelle, Léon, *Płonące Dusze* (Warsaw: Oficyna Wydawnicza Rekonkwista, 2011).

Delannoy, Abel, *Confession d'un SS* (unpublished typescript).

Devresse, Roland, *Les Volontaires de la Jeunesse a la Légion Wallonie*, Tome 14, *Battle of Pomérania* (unpublished typescript).

Devresse, Roland, *Les Volontaires de la Jeunesse a la Légion Wallonie* Tome 15, *The End on Oder* (unpublished typescript).

GéPé, *En Poméranie Coule l'Oder* (unpublished typescript).

Hellebaut, Frans, *La Drame de l'Europe de l'est* (unpublished typescript).

Jacques, Freddy, *Mémoires* (unpublished typescript).

Ladrière, Jean, *La Decision Politique en Belgique* (Bruxelles: Cahiers de la Fondation Nationale des Sciences Politiques, 1965).

Landwehr, Richard, *'Siegrunen Magazine'*, issue 80 (Meriam Press, Bennington, 2008).

Landwehr, Richard, Roba, Jean-Louis, Merriam, Ray, *The Wallonien – The History of the 5th SS-Sturmbrigade and 28th SS Volunteer Panzergrenadier Division* (Bennington VT: Meriam Press, 2006).

Littlejohn, David, *Foreign Legions of the Third Reich. Vol. 2: Belgium, Great Britain, Holland, Italy and Spain* (San Jose CA: James Bender Publishing, 1981).

Lumsden, Robin, *Waffen SS – Organizacja, Działania Bojowe, Umundurowanie* (Warsaw: Wydawnictwo Militaria, 1999).

Mabire, Jean, *Division de Choc Wallonie, Lutte á Mort en Poméranie* (Paris: ed. Jacques Grancher, 1996).

Martinez, Eduardo M. Gil, *The Spanish in the SS and Wehrmacht 1944–1945* (Atglen PA: Schiffer Publishing Ltd, 2012).

Michaelis, Rolf, *Nordland* (Warsaw: Wydawnictwo Militaria, 2004).

Norling, Erik, *The Story of a Spanish Waffen-SS Officer, SS-Obersturmführer R. Luis Garcia Valdajos* [in:] *Siegrunen Magazine #79* (Bennington VT: Meriam Press, 2007).

Régibeau, André, 'Je Veux Parler de Vous, Amis...' [in:] *Le témeraire*, nr 30, November/ December 1985.

Solarz, Jacek, *Wiking 1941-1945* (Warsaw: Wydawnictwo Militaria, 2003).

Steiner, Felix, *Ochotnicy Waffen SS. Idea i Poświęcenie* (Gdańsk: Oficyna Wydawnicza Finna, 2010).

Szutowicz, Andrzej, *Degrelle, Koniec Mitu, Czyli Tropem Walończyków i ich Wodza. Wyprawa na Lindenberg* (<http://www.pelczce.pl>) [date of access: 14/12/2012] .

Tatoń, Jerzy, 'Wojenne Okruchy', [in:] *'Stargardia'*, tome 2 (Stargard: Wyd. Musem in Stargard Szczeciński, 2002).

Tieke, Wilhelm, *Tragedy of the Faithful, a History of the III. (Germanisches) SS-Panzer Korps* (Winnipeg: Fedorowicz Publishing, 2001).

Williamson, Gordon, *The Waffen SS, 24 to 38 Divisions, & Volunteer Legions* (Oxford: Osprey Publishing, 2004).

Index

Index of German Military Formations

Index of General and Miscellaneous Terms